TREASURY'S PANEL MODEL FOR TAX ANALYSIS

by

James R. Nunns, Deena Ackerman, James Cilke
Julie-Anne Cronin*, Janet Holtzblatt, Gillian Hunter
Emily Lin, and Janet McCubbin

OTA Technical Working Paper 3

July 2008

OTA Technical Working Papers is an occasional series of reports on the research, models and datasets developed to inform and improve Treasury's tax policy analysis. Views and opinions expressed are those of the authors and do not necessarily represent official Treasury positions or policy. *OTA Technical Working Papers* are distributed in order to document OTA analytic methods and data and invite discussion and suggestions for revision and improvement. Comments are welcome and should be directed to the authors.

Office of Tax Analysis
U.S. Department of the Treasury
1500 Pennsylvania Avenue, NW
Washington, D.C. 20220

* U.S. Department of the Treasury. julie.anne.cronin@do.treas.gov

---

The authors are grateful to the staff of SOI and participants in the Tax Economist Forum for comments and suggestions. All the authors participated in building the Panel Model while working at the Office of Tax Analysis (OTA). Currently, James R. Nunns is the Director of Tax Policy for the New Mexico Taxation and Revenue Department. Deena Ackerman, Julie-Anne Cronin and Gillian Hunter are Financial Economists at OTA. James Cilke is a Senior Economist at the Joint Committee on Taxation. Janet Holtzblatt is a Senior Analyst with the Congressional Budget Office. Janet McCubbin is the Director of Economic Issues at the AARP Public Policy Institute. Emily Y. Lin was formerly a Financial Economist at OTA. The views expressed in this paper are those of the authors and do not necessarily represent those of the U.S. Department of the Treasury, the Joint Committee on Taxation, the Congressional Budget Office, the New Mexico Taxation and Revenue Department, or the AARP.

Table of Contents

TREASURY'S PANEL MODEL FOR TAX ANALYSIS

Synopsis

Over time an individual's demographic or economic status may change in ways that significantly change how they are affected by current or proposed federal tax laws. In addition, some provisions of the tax law have effects over multiple years, and the effects of some tax provisions change over time due to phase-ins, phase-outs, and other factors. Current economic analyses of the effect of federal tax laws are generally based on data from "cross-section" samples, so analyses capture the demographic and economic circumstances of individuals and the provisions of federal tax law only at a single point in time. Treasury's Office of Tax Analysis has developed a new model based on data from a "panel" sample that included the same individuals for 10 years. This model captures the changing demographic and economic circumstances of individuals and the effects of changes in tax law over the entire 10-year budget window. Analyses based on the model will provide policy makers and the general public a deeper understanding of the effects of current and proposed tax policies.

I. Introduction

Treasury's Office of Tax Analysis (OTA) and its counterparts in the Congress, the Joint Committee on Taxation (JCT) and the Congressional Budget Office (CBO), are responsible for providing policy makers with economic analyses of the effects of current and proposed federal tax law. Typical analyses address such issues as the effect of the law on government receipts, the effect on the distribution of the tax burden, and the effect on incentives to work, save, and engage in other economic activities. Until recently, these analyses have been based almost exclusively on data from "cross-section" samples, or models based on such data. A cross-section sample is one drawn from a population at a point in time, such as a sample of all tax returns filed in a particular year. Such samples are designed to accurately represent the characteristics of the population for the year or other point in time covered by the sample.

OTA, JCT, and CBO have routinely extrapolated cross-section samples so that they represent the population in each of a number of future years. These extrapolated cross-sections have allowed us to analyze the effects of changes in the tax law in each of these future years. Such extrapolations, however, do not allow us to analyze the effects of changes in the tax law on individuals over a period of time longer than a year, since in these extrapolated cross-sections an individual in the sample represents a different set of individuals in each year of the extrapolation. For example, if the sample is extrapolated over ten years, a 35-year old married man with two children and no sources of income other than wages in the first year still represents a 35-year old married man with two children and income solely from wages in the tenth year. The extrapolated cross-section will have a 45-year old male in the tenth year that represents the original 35-year old, but he will be an entirely different person, and no ten-year "history" will connect the two.

In addition, some provisions of the tax law have effects over multiple years and the effects of some tax provisions change over time due to phase-ins, sunsets, and other factors. Until recently, economic analyses of the effect of federal tax laws have been almost exclusively based on data from "cross-section" samples. Such analyses capture the demographic and economic circumstances of individuals and the provisions of federal tax law only at a single point in time, even though the actual provisions would not be well described by this snapshot.

To be able to analyze the effect of changes in tax law on individuals over time, each individual in the sample must represent the same set of individuals over time in the extrapolation. Also, for each individual we must know the changes in their demographic and economic characteristics in each year of the extrapolation period. Over time an individual's demographic or economic status may change in ways that significantly change how they are affected by current or proposed federal tax laws. We must know, for example, whether individuals change their dependency or marital status; have children and possibly other dependents of their own; enter and leave the workforce, perhaps permanently at retirement; change their patterns of consumption and savings; reallocate their assets; and relocate among local and state fiscal jurisdictions. Data on such demographic and economic changes must come from a "panel" sample, one in which the same individuals are sampled over multiple years.

Treasury's Office of Tax Analysis has developed a model based on data from a "panel" sample that included the same individuals for 10 years. Analyses based on OTA's panel model provide policy makers and the general public a more complete understanding of the effects of current and proposed tax policies. This model captures the changing demographic and economic circumstances of individuals and the effects of changes in tax law over the entire 10-year budget window. Ten year distributional analyses using Treasury's panel model were included in the final report of the 2005 Tax Reform Panel.[1]

Distributional analyses with models using multi-year data have been developed by Davies et al. (1984) and Fullerton and Rogers (1993). Their models used small samples of representative taxpayers to simulate lifetime paths of income and tax burdens. The model developed at OTA is based on a much larger and detailed panel data set and is capable of analyzing tax proposals in greater detail than these models, but covers a shorter time period than entire lifetimes. Unlike Fullerton and Rogers' model, the OTA panel model is not a general equilibrium model.

Three previous papers[2] have described the design of Treasury's new panel model and presented some preliminary distributional analyses and dynamic tabulations from the model. This paper builds on the three papers by providing greater detail on the development of the model as well as updated distributional and dynamic tabulation analyses. The paper is organized into six sections

---

[1] Report of the President's Advisory Panel on Federal Tax Reform, "Simple, Fair, and Pro-Growth: Proposals to Fix America's Tax System," November 2005, (http://www.taxreformpanel.gov/final-report/)

[2] See Cilke, et al. (2000), Cilke, et al. (2001), and Cronin et. al. (2003). All work on this project by James Cilke was performed while he was employed by OTA.

and includes five appendices. Section II describes the data used in the panel. Section III details the extrapolation methodology, including how it is updated for new assumptions and additional years. Sections IV and V describe the distributional and dynamic tabulation methodologies and analyses. Section VI concludes with an overview of the benefits as well as the limitations of the model.

The appendices include working papers that describe each component of the model building process. Appendix A describes the basic data including the 1987 to 1996 cohort panel (A1), the PSID (A2), and the estate tax data (A3). Appendix B describes the weighting of the refreshed panel. Appendix C describes the model's consumption (C1), higher education (C2), health insurance (C3), and transfer payment (C4) imputations. Appendix D describes the extrapolation (D1) and includes an algebraic description of the extrapolation (D2), a shortcut for updating the extrapolation (D3), and the methodology for extrapolating the estate tax (D3). Appendix E describes the equivalence scaling used in the model.

II. Data Used in the Model

A. <u>Data Requirements for a Panel Model</u>

The primary data source for representing the population in each year of the budget period in Treasury's new model is a ten-year panel sample of individual income tax returns. This panel consists of a "cohort" segment and a "refreshment" segment. The "cohort" segment represents all individuals in the population who were tax return filers or dependents of these filers in 1987, the initial year of the panel. The refreshment segment represents all individuals in the population who became non-dependent tax return filers after 1987, and their dependents. The panel thus represents the entire U.S. filing population in each of the ten years from 1987 through 1996 at the level of tax return units. It also contains annual links between dependent filers and their parents, so it is possible to form (tax) families in each year. The detailed information on income, deductions, exemptions, etc. required for distributing individual income tax burdens is included for each return in all years of the panel. The income information includes the components of capital income required for distributing the burden of the corporate income tax. The income information also includes most of the components required for constructing our economic welfare measure (discussed below).

The filing population, however, is not sufficient for all the analyses that OTA performs. In particular, distributional analyses present the distribution of all federal taxes, both current law and any law that might be proposed, for the entire U.S. population. For these analyses, the model needs a panel of permanent non-filers. This panel was imputed from the Panel Study of Income Dynamics (PSID).

All panel returns have also been linked to Form W-2 information, which provides earnings at the individual worker level, which is required for distributing payroll tax burdens within tax families for the analysis of marriage penalties (or bonuses) and similar equity considerations. Age and gender have been linked to the panel returns from Social Security administration data. Consumption, which is required for the distribution of excise taxes, has been imputed from the

Consumer Expenditure Survey. In addition, the tax calculators required to compute individual income tax liabilities under alternative tax laws have been developed for each year of the panel.

B. Cohort Panel

The panel model is based on data from several sources for the 10-year period 1987 through 1996. Most of the data are from tax and information returns filed with the IRS. The initial ("cohort") panel sample was designated from the individual income tax returns for tax year 1987 that were filed with IRS in 1988 and included in the annual cross section sample drawn by the Statistics of Income (SOI) Division in 1988. This sample consists of approximately 88,000 non-dependent tax returns. All non-dependent taxpayers, including secondary taxpayers on joint returns, who were represented in this 1987 sample were designated as members of the initial panel, as were all dependents of these taxpayers.[3] For the next nine years (i.e., through tax returns filed for tax year 1996), the SOI Division included in the initial panel sample any tax return filed that reported any panel member as a primary or secondary taxpayer. Estate tax data were collected for all members of the cohort panel for whom an estate tax return was filed.

C. Refreshment Panel

The initial panel sample represents the 1987 filing population, but it does not represent the filing population in subsequent years. Over time, the filing population grows, on net, due to immigration, dependents becoming non-dependents, and the movement of 1987 non-dependent non-filers into the filing population. To represent this growth in the filing population, the initial panel sample was supplemented with a "refreshment" panel of non-dependent filers who filed after 1987, and their dependents. The refreshment panel was constructed from the annual SOI cross section samples for tax years 1988 through 1996. The SOI samples for all these years included a simple random sample based on the same ending digits of Social Security numbers used by primary taxpayers. Primary taxpayers in this simple random sample in any year from 1988 through 1996 who were not in the initial sample for 1987 were designated as members of the refreshment sample and their returns filed in any subsequent tax year through 1996 were included in the refreshment panel.[4] SOI also obtained any estate tax return filed for any of these panel members who died between 1987 and 1996.

---

[3] Taxpayers and their dependents represented on returns for 1987 that were filed in subsequent years (through 1990) were also designated as members of the initial panel. With the addition of these late-filed returns, the initial panel sample represents the entire 1987 filing population.

[4] To calculate sample weights, it was necessary to determine which of the three groups a member of the refreshment panel belonged to because the groups represent different parts of the U.S. population. Non-dependent non-filers in 1987 (and their dependents) are part of the 1987 U.S. population that is not represented on 1987 tax returns, dependents of 1987 filers who subsequently become filers are part of the 1987 U.S. population and are represented on 1987 tax returns, and immigrants are not part of the U.S. population until the year of immigration. Age in 1987 and presence of pre-1987 earnings (both from Social Security Administration records) were used to determine which group refreshment panel members belonged to. Note that the refreshment panel is not a true panel because secondary taxpayers, including primary taxpayers who became secondary taxpayers (e.g., because they married), were not followed. Missing records were imputed to make this a true panel.

D. Permanent Non-Filers (PSID)

The initial and refreshment panels represent the population of individuals who were represented as a taxpayer or dependent on a return filed in any year between 1987 and 1996. The remainder of the U.S. population consists of those individuals who were never represented on a return between 1987 and 1996. The Panel Study of Income Dynamics (PSID) was used to represent this "permanent non-filer" segment of the population. The basic approach was to form tax units from PSID units, determine whether each tax unit was above or below the tax filing threshold in each year, and then select the units that were below the threshold in every year from 1987 through 1996.[5] These units form the basis of the permanent non-filer population. Together, the main sample, the refreshment sample, and the permanent non-filer sample form a panel roughly representative of the American population for the entire period (once weighted).

E. Information Return Data

For individuals represented on tax returns, wages reported on W-2 forms were available in all years and other income reported on 1099 forms was available in some years. The W-2 information was used to split earnings on joint returns, which is necessary for computing payroll taxes for each spouse and for use in analyzing marriage penalties and related issues. The W-2 information was also used in combination with 1099 information and PSID data to impute income for years in which the return unit did not file a return.

F. Estate Tax Data

Estate tax data for panel members who died and for whom an estate tax return was filed are included. Limited estate tax data for all panel members and more detailed data for most panel members were available. Beginning with filing year 1994, SOI included all panel members in the samples for the annual estate tax studies. Data collected for these studies include detailed information about assets owned by the decedent, liabilities and the estate tax calculation. Prior to 1994, the estate tax returns of panel members were included in the annual SOI studies only if they met the usual sampling criteria.[6] Most panel decedents met the sampling criteria and were included in the study. By the end of processing year 2000, over 6,000 estate tax returns had been filed for panel members; SOI data were available for 88 percent of these estates. Returns Transaction File (RTF) data were obtained for the remaining estates, which were primarily returns for smaller estates filed prior to 1994 that did not meet the regular SOI sampling criteria. The RTF data include taxable estate and subsequent tax calculations, but do not include total gross estate or deductions. Gross estate and deductions were imputed for panel members for whom only RTF records were available.

---

[5] The latest PSID year available was 1993 when this work was done, so the PSID file was extrapolated through 1996 using essentially the same methodology subsequently used to extrapolate the entire model. This methodology is described later in the paper.

[6] The SOI estate tax study is based on a stratified random sample of estate tax returns. Sample criteria include year of death, age, and gross estate.

G. Age and Gender

Individuals represented on tax returns were linked to Social Security administration records (the "DM-1 file) to obtain the date of birth, date of death, and gender of each person with a valid social security number (SSN) on every return. Ages for persons with missing SSNs were imputed to the extent possible.[7] Likewise, if the year-of-birth information obtained from the DM-1 was clearly wrong, the age was adjusted. For example, individuals on the panel are constrained to be under 107 years of age and non-dependent taxpayers and spouses are constrained to be at least 15 years old.

H. Imputations

The primary data described above either exclude or only partially include key variables that are required to measure economic welfare and tax burdens. There are four groups of these variables: consumption, education, health insurance and employer characteristics, and transfer payments. Imputations for each category were made for each individual in the tax return and PSID panels for all years.

Consumption. A family's share of consumption devoted to items subject to excise taxes needed to be imputed in order to measure the relative tax burden imposed on the consumption of these items. Consumption shares for these items were computed from the Consumer Expenditure Survey (CEX) conducted by the Bureau of Labor Statistics. We imputed 15 broad categories of expenditures as well as 3 subcategories of expenditures subject to excise. We also imputed smoking status and consumption using the National Institute of Health Survey. More detail on the data and methods used in these imputations is in Appendix C1.

Higher education. The status of late teens and adults as higher education students and the characteristics of the higher education institution a student attends were required to analyze the effect of the tax credits and above-the-line deduction for higher education. The 1995-1996 National Postsecondary Student Aid Study (NPSAS), produced by the Department of Education, provided information on a student's year in school, the degree program, whether the student was full-time or part-time, and the level and control of the institution the student was attending (e.g. public vs. private, 2-year vs. 4-year). Year-by-year profiles of a student's entire higher education status were constructed from the NPSAS. A separate tax data file was constructed for 1999 that provided information on the number of tax filers and dependents who were students, whether income-eligible students (or their parents, for dependent students) claimed the tax credit, an estimate of Pell grant or other aid, and whether a student attended an in-state or out-of-state institution. The NPSAS and 1999 tax files were statistically matched based on the age, marital status, family size and income of the student (or of the parents, for dependent students).

---

[7] In general, the imputed age of a married person was the age of his or her spouse. If the person claimed an extra elderly standard deduction, the imputed age was at least 65. If the return filed form 8615, the imputed age was under 14 years. The imputation of ages to dependents with missing SSNs depended on whether the person was missing in 1987 or not. Dependents first appearing after 1987 were usually given very low ages (0 or 1).

The combined matched NPSAS/1999 tax file was then statistically matched to the first year of the (extrapolated) panel (2004) based on age, earnings, total income, family size, dependency status, and status (for married students) as a primary or secondary filer. In this match, the weights from the 1999 tax records were exhausted, so that the panel had the target number of students. In each succeeding year of the panel a new match was performed to the combined matched NPSAS/1999 file to impute new beginning students. To be eligible for the match an individual on the panel could not be a student currently or have been a student in the preceding year. These matches hit separately generated targets for students by type of institution. A tuition level was then assigned to each student in each year, based on the type of institution, whether the student was in-state or out-of-state, and the year.

Health insurance. Health insurance coverage and premium amounts were imputed to the model to enable the model to analyze the effect of a wide variety of tax and health reform proposals. Employer-provided health coverage and tax preferred premium amounts were needed to be imputed to the model to analyze the effect of current law tax preferences. In addition, nongroup insurance coverage and premiums, out-of-pocket expenses, public coverage and uninsured status were needed to analyze the effects of reform proposals including exclusions and tax credits.

Because no single health survey includes the necessary items, several surveys were linked together through matching techniques. First data from the Robert Wood Johnson Employer Health Insurance Survey[8] (RWJ) were statistically matched using employer and employee characteristics to the Current Population Survey (CPS) to determine premiums, employer and employee contributions, and other plan characteristics for employer-provided health insurance. Then the CPS (with the matched RWJ plan variables) was matched to the panel in order to determine who is covered by employer, nongroup, Medicare and Medicaid health insurance and to identify the residual category of uninsured individuals. Nongroup health insurance premiums from the National Health Insurance Survey (NHIS) were assigned to individuals in the nongroup market. Finally, data from the Medical Expenditure Panel Survey (MEPS) were used to impute medical expenditures. Tax data already on the panel provided information on itemized medical expenses and the above-the-line deduction for health insurance for self-employed individuals.

Transfer payments. Cash income, the income concept used on the panel model, is the sum of income reported on income tax returns plus nontaxable cash transfer payments (including food stamps) and taxes excluded from income sources (the employer share of payroll taxes and the corporate income tax). Unemployment benefits and some Social Security benefits were reported on tax returns, and the remainder of Social Security benefits for filers was available in some years from forms 1099-SSA. Missing years of Social Security benefits were imputed, based on benefit levels in surrounding years. Social security and unemployment benefits were imputed to non-filers from the PSID, and other cash transfer payments (including food stamps) were imputed to filers from the PSID. Transfer payments by type were benchmarked to totals from administrative data for each program.

---

[8] Premiums from the employer survey in the MEPS were not used, because there was no way to link premiums to family income. The RWJ survey included both premiums and wage data, enabling a link since wages are the major component of income.

Detailed descriptions of the consumption, education, health insurance, and transfer payment imputations can be found in Appendix C.

III. Extrapolation

A. General Approach

The original panel data cover the 10-year period 1987-1996, and the budget period is also a 10-year period (currently, 2008-2017). The basic approach was to first divide the 1987 and 1996 non-dependent panel records into a number of matching cells and to align the income and weights within each 1987 cell with the income and weights in the corresponding 1996 cell. The records on the two files were then matched and the income adjustments from the 1987 records (now adjusted to 1996) carried forward to all years of the panel (which now represents 1996-2005). Finally, aggregate income by source was adjusted to actual or budget forecast targets. These steps were then repeated, with 1987 now matched to 2004 so that the extrapolated file covers the 2004-2013 budget period (the first budget period for which the model was in full production). The extrapolated file is then updated for population and income growth and adjusted to budget forecast targets each year so that it covers the current budget period (currently 2008-2017). A more detailed description follows.

B. Defining Cells

Seven variables define "super" matching cells, and each super matching cell was then divided into income and age ranking quantiles. The super matching cells were defined by marital status (single, married, head of household), three broad age groups, gender (for unmarried record units), second earner status (for married record units), number of dependents (none, one, two or more), filing status, and income type (six types that depend on the mix of income, e.g., one type requires that income is at least 90 percent wages and that losses from all sources are less than $3,000). Within each super cell in the 1996 file, all (weighted) records were then ranked into income quantiles. Each quantile was required to have at least 10 unweighted records, or the quantile was collapsed into surrounding quantiles. Income from each source on the records in the corresponding super cell on the 1987 file was then grown by the ratio of the super-cell average for the source on the 1996 file to the corresponding super-cell average for the source on the 1987 file. Total (grown) income was then computed for each 1987 record, and the 1987 file divided into income cells using the dollar quantile breaks from the 1996 file. Within each income cell, age quantiles were then computed for each file, and the smaller number of breaks (based on the requirement of at least 10 unweighted records in each cell on each file) was used to define the age cells within the income cells.[9] The final step before performing the match was to proportionately adjust the weights within each cell on the 1987 file so that the total of the record weights matched the total of the record weights in the corresponding cell in the 1996 file.

---

[9] The preceding steps resulted in some cells with fewer than 10 unweighted observations. These cells were collapsed into surrounding cells. The process of defining age quantiles was repeated using adjusted income on the 1987 file to improve file alignment.

C. Matching at the Micro Level

For the match, records within each cell on both files were sorted by income and age, so the first (top income) record from the 1987 file was linked to the first (top income) record on the 1996 file. If the (adjusted) weight of the matched 1987 record exceeded the weight of the matched 1996 record, the weight of the 1987 record was reduced by the weight of the 1996 record, and the 1987 record was reused in the next match. Otherwise, the 1987 record kept its (remaining) weight and the next 1987 record was matched to the same 1996 record, taking its remaining weight (or some of it). This process continued until all 1987 records were matched (which meant all the 1996 records had been matched also, since the two files had identical total weights within each cell).

D. Hitting Aggregate Targets

The next step was to make final adjustments to income items and to adjust the level of deductions on the 1987 records. The level of total (grown) income on each 1987 record was first adjusted to the total income on the matched 1996 record.[10] Then, each amount of income from each source was adjusted so that the total amount from that source on the 1987 file matched the total amount from the 1996 file. The growth in total income (or, total income excluding capital gains) from the original 1987 amount on each extrapolated 1987 record was used to adjust itemized deductions. The amount of each extrapolated itemized deduction on each record was then adjusted so the total amount on all records hit known 1996 targets.

Once the extrapolation of non-dependent 1987 records was completed, adjustment factors (the ratio of the extrapolated 1996 amount to the original 1987 amount) were computed for each income source and deduction for each record. These adjustment factors were then applied to each subsequent year of the extrapolated file, including returns filed by dependents, to give an initial extrapolation to the 1996-2005 period. The final step was to proportionately adjust each income and deduction item on each record for each year so that the aggregate amount hit known (or forecast) targets. Since the targets are for filers, the filing status of records was determined and the initial adjustment applied only to filers.[11] The same adjustment factors were then applied to items on non-filer records. This resulted in a final extrapolated file for the 1996-2005 period.

E. Second Extrapolation

The second extrapolation followed the same procedure described above, with the 1987 file matched to the 2004 extrapolated file, resulting ultimately in the 2004-2013 extrapolated file

---

[10] Adjustment factors were capped above at 10 and below at 0.1.

[11] Filing status was first determined by comparing the record's income to the filing threshold for the filing status, eligibility for refundable credits, presence of wages, and other indicators of filing. Records just above or below filing based on these indicators were then brought into or moved out of filing status to hit a target for the total number of filers for the year. Another round of adjustments might be required after incomes, etc. were adjusted to targets.

used to produce the simulations reported in this paper.[12] Because records were split in both stages of the extrapolation, the number of records in the model increased from 1.4 million in the initial 1987-1996 file to 3.9 million in the 2004-2013 extrapolated file.

F. Updating the Extrapolation

The current base extrapolation (for 2004-2013) is updated twice each year. The two updates follow the same methodology except that the first update uses winter Budget assumptions and the second is based on Mid-Session Review assumptions.[13] The first update also moves the Budget window one year forward to the current Budget window (e.g. from 2007-2016 to 2008-2017) and increases the return weights. A step-by-step algebraic description of the "short-cut" method for updating the extrapolation is given in Appendix D3.

In brief, the short-cut extrapolation proceeds as follows. Each income item on each return is grown by the aggregate rate of growth for that income item, where the initial amount of aggregate income for an item is the sum for that item across all returns as measured in the current base extrapolation and the target amount as given by the winter Budget (or Mid-Session Review) assumptions. For example, for the 2008-2017 winter Budget (WB08) update, if the target amount of wages for 2008 as given by the WB08 assumptions is x percent higher than the sum of all wages in 2004 as measured in the current base extrapolation, then wages for every 2004 return would be increased by x percent to update it to 2008 levels.

Exogenous non-income items (e.g. itemized deductions) for each return are first grown by the return's forecasted rate of growth of total income (either with or without capital gains[14]). For example, if a return's total income with capital gains in 2008 as calculated using the income growth factors (above) is y percent greater than it was in 2004 as measured under the current base extrapolation, then charitable contributions are first grown by y percent. Most itemized deductions are then adjusted for aggregate forecasted differential rates of growth for the deduction relative to total income (or total income without gains). For example, if on average charitable contributions are expected to grow slightly slower than total income between 2004 (as measured by the current base extrapolation) and 2008 (as forecast) then charitable contributions on all returns for 2008 would be lowered by the ratio of the average growth rate for charitable contributions over the average growth rate for total income between 2004 and 2008.

IV. Distributional Analysis with the Model

The panel model has allowed OTA to extend its distributional analysis from a single year to a multi-year period. We can use a multi-year measure of income to rank families, and calculate a multi-year measure of tax burdens. In contrast to the single-year measure, our multi-year

---

[12] Estate tax returns are extrapolated separately, using the general methodology Treasury uses to extrapolate the estate tax file used for revenue estimating purposes. See Appendix D4.

[13] Updated transfer targets are generally not available in time for the winter Budget update.

[14] See Appendix D3 for a complete list of relevant growth factors.

measure of income allows us to capture some lifecycle effects, better measure temporary relative to permanent changes in demographic and economic circumstances, and more accurately rank savers and non-savers. It also allows us to better measure the burden of temporary provisions and provisions with unindexed parameters.

For example, workers typically have lower wages when they are young than they will earn later in their working lives, and have no earnings when they retire. Likewise, current earnings might rank an individual temporarily out of work too low in terms of longer term welfare and current income might lead to too high a ranking if an individual has a one-time large capital gains realization.

In contrast to our single-year measure of tax burdens, our multi-year measure of tax burdens captures tax laws that follow lifecycle patterns, have multiple year effects, or that are temporary, phase in over time or are not indexed for inflation. For example, a proposed child credit would not be shown to benefit a childless couple if only their current demographic circumstances were taken into account, but the couple would benefit if they had children in a subsequent year. Payroll taxes only apply to current workers, but they would affect a young student who was about to enter the labor force, and they did affect the retiree during the years he or she was in the labor force.

Other provisions have multiple-year effects. These include the deduction or exclusion of contributions to IRAs and other retirement plans, the inside buildup on retirement plan contributions which is taxed upon withdrawal, and the deferral of tax on unrealized capital gains. A sunset provision will effectively repeal the tax cuts enacted under the Economic Growth and Tax Relief Reconciliation Act of 2001 (EGTRRA) and the Jobs and Growth Tax Relief Reconciliation Act of 2003 (JGTRRA) in 2010. Because the AMT exemption amount is not indexed for inflation, many more taxpayers will be affected each year. A multi-year measure can evaluate such provisions on a year-by-year basis, and therefore fully reflect their effects throughout the period.

A. Methodology Summary

The panel model allows Treasury to extend the time period of analysis to a multi-year period, but the objective of our distributional methodology is otherwise unchanged from the single-year: to provide a comprehensive measure of the effect of current and proposed tax laws on the distribution of tax burdens. Implementing that objective in a multi-year context leads us to the following choices in each dimension of distributional analysis.

Taxes included. As under our single-year methodology, [15] all federal taxes are included.

Incidence assumptions. These are unchanged from the single-year methodology.

Time period of analysis. The time period of analysis will be the ten-year budget period that begins in the succeeding calendar year. For example, the current budget period is 2008 through

---

[15] See "U.S. Treasury Distributional Analysis Methodology" (Cronin, 1999; http://www.treas.gov/offices/tax-policy/library/ota85.pdf) for a complete description of Treasury's single year methodology.

2017. The same period will be used for the measurement of income and for the measurement of tax burdens.

Unit of analysis. Family membership in many cases changes over the ten-year budget period. The basic unit of analysis over the budget period must therefore be individuals. In each year of the budget period, as explained below, cash income and tax burdens are first computed at the family level, and then allocated to individuals. These individual-level results are then annuitized to display the results.

Ranking individuals by multi-year cash income. In each year of the ten-year budget period, the annual cash income of each family is measured, adjusted for family size (see Equivalence Scales below), and then allocated to each individual member of the family. Thus each individual present in the first year of the budget period will have a size adjusted value of cash income for every year of the budget period.[16] The level real annuity equivalent of these individual streams of cash income over the budget period is then calculated and individuals are ranked by this measure into quintiles or fixed dollar classes. Each of these steps is discussed in some detail below.

Tax burden measures. The steps involved are similar to those used for ranking families by income. In each year of the ten-year budget period, the tax burden of each family in that year under current law and under proposed law is computed, using the relevant tax law in effect in that year. These tax burdens are then adjusted for family size, and allocated to each individual member of the family. The level annuity equivalent of each individual's stream of tax burdens over the budget period is then calculated.

B. Measuring Welfare

OTA assumes that all family members in a given year have equal welfare. Families are assumed to act as an economic unit, sharing both resources and costs. This is implicit in OTA's single year income measure and also applies to the multi-year measure. The sources of income do not matter in assigning income to family members. For example, if all family income is derived from the earnings of one member, that member is still assigned the same level of welfare as the non-working members. Likewise, tax burdens are assumed to be shared equally among family members.

Cash income is used as a proxy for welfare. An important difference between income and welfare measures is that an income measure omits the value of leisure time. If two otherwise identical families (or individuals) have the same wage income but have different levels of work effort, they will have the same rank under an income measure even though their welfare is obviously not equivalent.

Another important difference is that welfare measures control for differences in prices faced by consumers. If two otherwise identical families have the same income but one lives in a high cost-of-living area, the two families would have the same rank under an income measure even

---

[16] Individuals who die during the Budget period will have fewer than ten years of income. The present value and annuity formulas are adjusted accordingly.

though the purchasing power of the family living in the high cost of living area is considerably lower. Finally, forward-looking welfare measures consider the degree of uncertainty surrounding earnings and consumption choices; income measures do not.

OTA's choice of income as a proxy for welfare is based on several considerations. Although income may not be a good proxy for welfare in some instances, income is measured with a relatively high degree of precision whereas the value of leisure, the prices faced by different families, and uncertainty of income and consumption streams could only be measured with imprecision. Further, income is a more familiar concept than welfare and therefore may better convey relative rankings to policy makers.

Cash income. Cash income includes wages and salaries[17], net income from a business or farm, taxable and tax-exempt interest, dividends, rental income, realized capital gains, cash transfers from the government, and retirement benefits. Employer contributions for payroll taxes and the federal corporate income tax are added to place cash income on a pre-tax basis. Annual cash income is measured on a family rather than on a tax return basis. The cash incomes of all members of a family in a single year are added to arrive at a family's annual cash income. This annual measure is then adjusted for family size, and each family member is allocated the size adjusted level of cash income for their family in that year. For example, if in 2008 the Smiths are a family of three with two adults and one minor child where one adult earns $50,000 and there is no other cash income, then the Smith's size-adjusted family cash income is $31,867 (family size adjustments are described below). This amount is assigned to each of the three individuals in the family for 2008.

Equivalence scales. The multi-year period of OTA's new distributional analyses necessitates an explicit adjustment for family size. In these multi-year analyses, the income and tax burdens of base-year families are measured over the ten-year budget period. Because family composition changes over the budget period, a base-year *family's* income and tax burden cannot be measured in each year of the budget period. Instead, the income and tax burdens for each *individual* who existed in the base year are measured in each year. The equivalence scale used for this measure determines how a family's income is translated into the income of each individual in the family in each year. If the equivalence scale assumed perfect returns to scale, each individual in a given family in a given year would be assigned the family's income for that year. At the other extreme, if the equivalence scale assumed no returns to scale then the family's income in each year would be divided by the number of individuals in the family. OTA's equivalence scale falls between these two extremes.

The specific equivalence scale we have chosen adjusts for family size (i.e., for economies of scale as family size increases), but not for other economic or demographic differences among families. The scale was derived from the official U.S. poverty levels by computing the coefficient on the size of the family that yields the same scale as the U.S. poverty levels for

---

[17] Fringe benefits are not included in cash income.

families of one and three persons.[18] We chose this scale because it closely matches utility-based scales found in the literature, and it is straightforward to compute for any family size. It also approximates the U.S. poverty thresholds for most people.[19] See Appendix E for more information on equivalence scales.

Annuitization. As discussed above, OTA measures cash income over multiple years, adjusts each family's cash income for family size in each year of the budget period, and allocates the adjusted amount to each individual in the family. This gives us a stream of adjusted cash income over the budget period for each individual present in the first year of the budget period. We perform similar calculations to arrive at each individual's tax burden streams. We then annuitize the ten year streams of income and taxes in order to arrive at a summary measure of an individual's "ten year" income and tax burden.

The annuitization process works as follows. For purposes of illustration, we limit the discussion to the calculation of the level annuity of income. The calculation of the level annuity of tax burden is analogous. For each individual present in the first year of the budget period, we calculate the present discounted value of each individual's equivalenced income stream using the actual inflation rate as measured by the CPI-U and an assumed real rate of interest of 4 percent. Then, we calculate the level real annuity over the budget period that has the same present discounted value as the equivalenced income stream for each individual present in the first year of the budget period. OTA uses the actual expected inflation rates[20] in each year of the budget period but if the inflation rate were constant, the annuity formula would appear as follows:

$$A_i = \frac{\left[1 - \left(\frac{1+\pi}{1+R}\right)\right] * PDV(C\_I_i)}{\left[1 - \left(\frac{1+\pi}{1+R}\right)^{N(i)}\right]}$$

where:

i   indexes individual members of the sample;

A_i =   the level annuity value of income for individual i;

_____

[18] The coefficient is called the "family size elasticity" (fse). The fse in the equivalence scale we use (.41) was derived from the U.S. poverty levels for one and three person families in 1998 ($8,316 and $13,003, respectively) by solving the following formula: $\$8,316/1^{fse} = \$13,003/3^{fse}$.

[19] By design, OTA's equivalence scale exactly matches the poverty thresholds for families of size 1 and 3, and it closely matches the poverty threshold for families of size 2. Ninety percent of all families in 2000 were made up of 1, 2, or 3 members. A constant FSE of .41 does not approximate the U.S. poverty thresholds for large families. A much higher FSE would be necessary to capture the large additional amounts of income allowed large families under the poverty thresholds.

[20] Expected inflation rates are the same as those used for revenue estimating purposes and are updated twice annually for winter budget and the Mid-Session Review.

π = the assumed constant rate of inflation;

R = an assumed nominal interest rate such that the real interest rate equals 4%;

N(i) = a count of the years individual i appeared in the sample, and

$PDV(C\_I_i)$ is the present discounted value of cash income for individual i over the budget period.

C. Measuring Consumption

Shares of consumption devoted to items subject to excise taxes are required to estimate the distributional effect of these taxes.[21] Consumption shares for these items were computed from the Consumer Expenditure Survey (CEX) conducted by the Bureau of Labor Statistics. To obtain a sufficiently large sample from the CEX, all consumer units reporting in the first quarter of the 1995 and 1996 surveys were used. Units that did not report in all four quarters were matched to similar units and the missing quarters of expenditures imputed, so that all units had a full year of expenditures. Expenditures for each unit were then divided between durables and non-durables, and the share of non-durable expenditures was computed for each item subject to an excise. Seven matching variables for the resulting CEX file and each year of the panel file were then computed: family type (four categories), age of unit head, gender of unmarried unit heads, number of children, number of adults other than the head and spouse, consumption centile, and presence of a smoker. On the panel, consumption was defined as after-tax (cash) income.[22] Smoking status was imputed to all individuals over age 13 in all years of the panel, based on the probability of smoking by age, income quantile, and marital status from the National Institute of Health survey.

The initial match of the CEX was to the 1987 panel file. A penalty function was used to insure that only similar units were matched. A panel unit (a "tax family") retained its consumption shares from the initial match in subsequent years unless its family type changed, its current income rank was more than 10 centiles away from its 1987 rank, or it changed smoking status. If any of these three changes occurred in a year, the unit was re-matched to the CEX file to obtain new consumption shares. See appendix C1 for more information on the consumption imputation.

---

[21] See Cronin (1999; http://www.treas.gov/offices/tax-policy/library/ota85.pdf) for a description of the basic methodology Treasury uses to distribute excise taxes and customs duties.

[22] Note that cash income many types of savings including: contributions to 401(k) type accounts, inside build up on tax preferred savings vehicles, and accrued capital gains (including housing capital gains). Net capital losses were capped at $50,000 in the computation of consumption. In addition, a lower bound was imposed on consumption of half the poverty level for a single individual, with this amount adjusted for larger families using the family equivalence scale. An upper bound on consumption of $5 million was also imposed.

D. Measuring Taxes

Distributional analysis on the panel model begins with the distribution of each tax to tax families in each year. A tax family is defined as the non-dependent primary taxpayer, the taxpayer's spouse, and their dependents for income tax purposes. Individual income tax liabilities are distributed to payers (which includes dependent filers), payroll taxes to individual workers, corporate income to capital income generally, excises taxes to families according to their consumption patterns and their total labor and capital income, and the estate and gift taxes to decedents. Tax liabilities, by tax, are aggregated at the family level. Family-level income and tax liabilities in each year are then divided by an equivalence scale and assigned to each individual in the family.

E. Illustration: Tax Burdens under Current Law

As measured above, each individual present in the first year of the budget period has a stream of income and tax liabilities for each year he or she is present in the panel. Annuity equivalent streams of income and tax burdens are then calculated and used in the ten year distribution tables produced by Treasury. Table 1 below shows the percent distribution of individual annuitized cash income and federal taxes by type over the budget period (2007-2016) under policy baseline law.[23]

As discussed above, although we assume that families share income and tax burdens in a particular year, only individuals can be followed over time. Table 1 therefore distributes *individual* income and tax burdens. Every individual in the U.S. population in the first year of the budget period (including children) is included in the table. If a family maintains the same membership across all ten years (i.e. no births, deaths, marriages or divorces, and no children that become non-dependents), then all members of the family will be ranked exactly the same in the table. In all other cases, each member will have a ranking that reflects his or her income or tax burdens over time. For example, if a family composed of a husband and wife in year 1 is divorced in year 5 and both remarry in year 7, then their ranking will be a weighted average of their incomes under both marriages and the time during which they were single. Likewise, if a

---

[23] Policy baseline law assumes the tax cuts enacted by EGTRRA and JGTRRA are extended. Note that the estate tax is repealed under fully phased in policy baseline law.

Table 1
Distribution of Individuals, Annuitized Individual Cash Income, and Federal Taxes Over the Budget Period under Policy Baseline Law[1]

(Annuitized Individual Ten Year Income Levels and Taxes)

Annuitized Individual Ten Year Cash Income Quintile	Individuals	Annuitized Individual Ten Year Cash Income	Total Federal Taxes	Individual Income Taxes	Corporate Income Taxes	Payroll Taxes	Excises & Customs Duties	Estate
--- Percent Distribution ---								
Lowest[2]	19.8	3.1	0.4	-1.3	0 6	2.7	2 0	0.1
Second	20.0	7 6	3.8	0.1	2 2	9.4	6 9	1.0
Third	20.0	13 0	10.3	6.0	6.1	17.6	13 2	0.7
Fourth	20.0	20 5	19.8	16.2	13.7	26.9	21 0	0.4
Highest	20.0	56 2	65.6	78.9	77 0	43.4	56 9	97.0
Total[2]	100.0	100 0	100.0	100.0	100 0	100.0	100 0	100.0
Top 10	10.0	41 2	49.3	63.2	65 0	25.0	41 3	88.9
Top 5	5.0	30.7	37.5	50.2	54 2	14.4	30 6	83.3
Top 1	1.0	16 6	20.8	29.1	35 5	4.5	16.4	58.3
--- As a Percent of Income ---								
Lowest[2]			3.2	-5.5	0.5	7.5	0 6	0.00
Second			12.5	0.1	0 8	10.7	0 9	0.01
Third			19.6	5.8	1.2	11.6	1 0	0.00
Fourth			24.1	10.0	1.8	11.3	1 0	0.00
Highest			29.0	17.7	3.6	6.6	1 0	0.1
Total[2]			24.8	12.6	2.7	8.6	1 0	0.04
Top 10			29.8	19.3	4 2	5.2	1 0	0.1
Top 5			30.3	20.6	4.7	4.0	1 0	0.1
Top 1			31.3	22.1	5.7	2.3	1 0	0.1

Department of the Treasury
Office of Tax Analysis

[1] The Policy Baseline assumes the current law tax cuts are extended.

[2] Families with negative incomes are excluded from the lowest income quintile but included in the total line.

NOTE: Quintiles begin at individual annuity equivalent income of: Second $15,216; Third $29,612; Fourth $47,663; Highest $75,223; Top 10% $105,510; Top 5% $146,840; Top 1% $349,780.

couple with one child remains married for ten years but their child leaves the family after five years, the two adult members will have the same rank but their child will have a different rank that will reflect his or her years as a non-dependent. Further, if the couple has the same income in the years with and without the child, their individual adjusted income in the years without the child will be higher to reflect the fact that their real income is higher.[24]

Although individuals who are not part of the U.S. population in the first year of the budget period are not explicitly included in the table, births and immigration (like deaths and emigration) will affect the measurement of income and tax burdens either directly by generating

---

[24] Note that the increase in income due to having one less family member will be relatively small due to the assumed returns to scale for family size. For example, if the family's income were $100,000 (with and without the child), each individual in the family would be assigned an income of $63,735 in the case with the child and $75,262 without the child.

income or tax liabilities in the succeeding years, or indirectly through their impact on equivalence scales or the application of tax law (e.g. child tax credits).

The ten-year distributions of income and tax burdens in Table 1 show that policy baseline law is progressive. The lowest quintile of individuals has an total federal effective tax rate of 3.2%; the second lowest quintile has an effective tax rate of 12.5% and the middle quintile has an effective rate of 19.6%. The second highest quintile has an effective rate of 24.1% and the top quintile has an effective rate of 29.0%.

The top quintile's share of ten-year income is 56.2% and their share of the ten year measure of total federal tax burden is 65.6. In contrast, the lowest quintile's share of income is 3.1% and their share of total federal taxes is 0.4%.

The individual income tax is the largest federal tax, just over half of all federal tax burdens. It is also very progressive. Because of refundable individual income tax credits, the lowest quintile's effective individual income tax rate is -5.5% under the ten year tables. The second quintile of individuals bears almost no individual income tax burden and the middle quintile's effective individual income tax rate is only 5.8%. In contrast, the effective individual income tax rate is 10.0% for the second highest quintile, 17.7% for the highest quintile, and 22.1% for the top 1%.

After the individual income tax, the payroll tax is the next largest federal tax, almost 35% of the total federal tax burden. Payroll tax burdens are progressive through the third quintile, flatten out and then become regressive. This pattern is explained by two factors. First, only earned income is subject to payroll taxation and the composition of income changes as we move up the income distribution. Lower income individuals tend to have relatively more transfer and other non-wage income; middle income taxpayers tend to have mostly earned income; and higher income taxpayers have increasingly more capital income. Second, the FICA/SECA portion of the payroll tax is capped at relatively high earnings.

The corporate income tax is the third largest federal tax, accounting for almost 11% of the total tax burden. Like the individual income tax, most of the burden of the corporate income tax is borne by higher income taxpayers. In contrast, excises and customs (4% of total federal tax burdens) are fairly flat. The estate tax is the most progressive tax in the table but it accounts for very little of the tax burden (0.2%) because it is phased out by 2010.

F. Illustration: Comparison to Single-Year Table

Table 2 shows distributional results comparable to Table 1, but estimated using the single-year methodology and assuming fully phased in policy baseline law at 2007 levels of income. [25] As expected the ten-year table (Table 1) has relatively flatter distributions of both income and total tax burdens. Because the ten-year tables "average" good years with bad years, the extremes that may be present in a single-year table are smoothed out. For example, if a person realizes a large amount of capital gains in a particular year they might appear to be higher income in a single year table than they would in a multi-year table. Likewise a person might have a short spell of

---

[25] Fully phased in policy baseline law excludes temporary provisions (ignoring the EGTRRA and JGTRRA sunsets) and adjusts for the effects of unindexed parameters.

low income during college years or unemployment spells but might have higher wages in other years.

Family Cash Income Quintile	Families	Family Cash Income	Total Federal Taxes	Individual Income Taxes	Corporate Income Taxes	Payroll Taxes	Excises & Customs Duties	Estate
--- Percent Distribution ---								
Lowest[2]	19.5	2 0	0.3	-0.7	0.3	2.0	1 0	0.0
Second	20.0	6.1	2.2	-1.2	1.6	5.9	4 5	0.0
Third	20.0	11 6	8.1	3.7	5.1	14.1	10 8	0.0
Fourth	20.0	20.1	18.1	14.0	13.7	24.9	19 8	0.0
Highest	20.0	60 9	71.3	84.2	79.1	53.0	63.7	0.0
Total[2]	100.0	100 0	100.0	100.0	100.0	100.0	100 0	0.0
Top 10	10.0	45.1	54.4	68.6	68.7	32.5	47.4	0.0
Top 5	5.0	33 9	41.3	54.9	59.9	18.8	35 6	0.0
Top 1	1.0	18 8	22.7	31.8	42.5	5.4	19.7	0.0
--- As a Percent of Income ---								
Lowest[2]			3.7	-3.8	0.4	9.1	0 5	
Second			8.8	-2.4	0.7	9.0	0.7	
Third			17.3	3.8	1.2	11.2	0 9	
Fourth			22.4	8.3	1.8	11.4	0 9	
Highest			29.0	16.5	3.5	8.0	1 0	
Total[2]			24.8	12.0	2.7	9.2	1 0	
Top 10			30.0	18.2	4.1	6.7	1 0	
Top 5			30.3	19.4	4.8	5.1	1 0	
Top 1			29.9	20.2	6.1	2.6	1 0	

Table 2
Distribution of Families, Cash Income, and Federal Taxes under Fully Phased In Policy Baseline Law[1]

(Fully phased in Law at 2007 Income Levels)

Department of the Treasury
Office of Tax Analysis

[1] The Policy Baseline assumes the current law tax cuts are extended.

[2] Families with negative incomes are excluded from the lowest income quintile but included in the total line.

NOTE: Quintiles begin at cash income of: Second $13,310; Third $28,507; Fourth $50,448; Highest $87,758; Top 10% $128,676; Top 5% $177,816; Top 1% $432,275.

The highest income quintile's share of the single-year cash income is 60.9% compared to 56.2% in the ten-year table. The bottom quintile's share of income is 2.0% in the single-year table compared to 3.1% in the ten year tables. The highest income quintile's share of the single-year total federal tax burdens is 71.3% compared to 65.6% in the ten-year table. The bottom quintile's share of total federal tax burdens is 0.3% in the single-year table compared to 0.4% in the ten-year table.

Because the distribution of both income and tax burdens are flatter in the ten-year tables, the difference in effective rates between the two tables depends on what happens to the relative shares of income and tax burdens between the two tables. For the top quintile the relative shares move together and the effective rate for total federal taxes is the same in the ten-year and single-year tables. For the lowest quintile the effective rate is lower in the ten-year tables. This is not surprising since these are individuals who are consistently ranked low and are eligible for refundable individual income tax credits in multiple years. All other quintiles have higher effective rates in the ten-year table than in the single-year table. The top 1% also has a higher effective rate in the ten-year table.

The individual income tax appears more progressive in the ten-year table, ranging from an effective tax rate of -5.5% for the lowest quintile to 22.1% for the top 1%, compared to an effective tax rate of -3.8% for the lowest quintile and 20.2% for the top 1% in the single-year table.

G. Illustration: Distributional Analysis of Recent Legislation

Table 3 provides two measures of the results of the distributional analysis of recent legislation. The top panel of Table 3 shows the percent of total tax liabilities by income quintile. The bottom panel of Table 3 shows by income quintile effective tax rates, indexed to the average effective rate for the tax law. Indexed rates isolate how the relative tax burdens of different income groups have been affected by the changes in the various tax laws.

Several legislative trends are apparent from both measures presented in Table 3. First, every major tax law, if in effect over the entire 2004-2013 budget period, would have reduced the relative tax burdens on individuals in the first three income quintiles, with a large cumulative effect between TRA86 law and EGTRRA plus JGTRRA law. These relative reductions are due primarily to the expansions of the EITC, the adoption and expansion of the child tax credit and its refundability feature, and the new 10 percent bracket. Second, the fourth income quintile would have had a cumulative reduction in relative tax burdens since TRA86 by either measure, but the pattern is mixed, with relative reductions through OBRA93 and relative increases subsequently. Third, relative tax burdens on individuals in the highest income quintile would have been increased by every major law since TRA86. These relative net tax increases are due primarily to increases in individual income tax rates (but, not in EGTRRA and JGTRRA).

The panel model provides a 10-year, forward-looking dimension to the distributional effects of federal tax laws. A different dimension is provided by analyses based on cross-section models. For example, the Congressional Budget Office (CBO) has periodically published its analysis of the distribution of federal taxes in effect in selected prior years.[26] CBO's analyses capture the combined effects of historical changes in the tax laws and in the demographic and economic circumstances of households between years. Such retrospective analyses inform policy makers and the general public about actual historical developments in federal tax policy, which shape perspectives on future tax policies.

---

[26] See CBO (2006), "Historical Effective Tax Rate: 1979 to 2004," (http://www.cbo.gov/ftpdocs/77xx/doc7718/EffectiveTaxRates.pdf).

Income Quintile[4]	TRA 86	OBRA 90	OBRA 93	TRA97 Fully Phased In	EGTRRA and JGTRRA As Enacted	EGTRRA and JGTRRA Without Phase-ins	EGTRRA and JGTRRA Without Phase-ins or Sunsets	EGTRRA and JGTRRA Without Phase-ins, Sunsets or AMT
					--- Percent Distribution ---			
Lowest[5]	1.0	0.9	0.6	0.5	0.4	0.4	0.4	0.4
Second	4.8	4.7	4.2	4.1	3.9	3.8	3.8	3.9
Third	10.7	10.6	10 1	10.0	10.0	10.0	10.0	10 2
Fourth	19.5	19.4	18.6	18.8	18.9	19.1	19.3	19.4
Highest	63.7	64.2	66 2	66.4	66.6	66.5	66.4	65 9
Total[5]	100.0	100.0	100.0	100.0	100.0	100.0	100.0	100.0
Top 10	47.7	48.3	50 9	50.9	50.9	50.7	50.3	49.8
Top 5	36.2	36.9	39.7	39.6	39.4	39.1	38.6	38 2
Top 1	20.1	20.6	23 1	22.9	22.6	22.3	21.7	21 9
					--- Indexed Effective Rate ---			
Lowest[5]	32.0	29.0	17.9	16.6	13.7	12.6	11.5	11.9
Second	62.4	60.7	54.8	52.6	50.1	49.4	48.7	50.2
Third	81.4	80.5	76.6	75.9	75.6	75.6	75.9	77.6
Fourth	95.3	94.5	90.9	91.5	92.3	93.0	94.0	94.9
Highest	114.2	115.1	118.8	119.1	119.4	119.3	119.1	118 1
Total[5]	100.0	100.0	100.0	100.0	100.0	100.0	100.0	100.0
Top 10	117.3	118.8	125.2	125.1	125.1	124.5	123.7	122.3
Top 5	119.9	121.9	131.4	130.8	130.4	129.2	127.5	126.2
Top 1	124.0	127.5	142.9	141.6	139.7	137.5	134.0	135.2

[1] The calculations are based on a representative sample of individual income tax returns filed over the 10-year period 1987 through 1996 and a sample of nonfilers taken from the Panel Survey on Income Dynamics (PSID) The combined samples have been extrapolated to the Budget period, 2004-2013

[2] The taxes included are individual and corporate income, payroll (Social Security and unemployment), excises, customs duties, and estate and gift taxes The individual income tax is assumed to be borne by payers, the corporate income tax by capital generally, payroll taxes (employer and employee shares) by labor (wages and self-employment income), excises on purchases by individuals in proportion to relative consumption of the taxed good and proportionately by labor and capital income and excises on purchases by businesses and customs duties proportionately by labor and capital income, and the estate and gift taxes by decedents

[3] Income and tax liabilities over the Budget period (2004-2014) are on an annuitized, family-equivalenced basis for each individual present in the first year of the Budget period (2004) All individual members of a family in a year are assumed to share equally in the family's income and tax liabilities for the year Each family's income and tax liabilities for a year is divided by an equivalence scale and these equivalenced amounts are assigned to each member of the family The equivalence scale increases with the size of the family and is related to the official poverty thresholds Dividing by the equivalence scale is necessary to put the income and tax liabilities of individuals in families of different sizes on a comparable basis The year-by-year amounts of each individual's income and tax liabilities are then converted to their present value in the first year of the Budget period Each present value amount is then converted to the level real annuity over the Budget period with the same present value

[4] The income measure is individual annuitized cash equivalent income It is a summary measure of an individual's cash income over the Budget period (see footnote 3) Cash income consists of wages and salaries, net income from a business or farm, taxable and tax-exempt interest, dividends, rental income, realized capital gains, cash transfers from the government, and retirement benefits Employer contributions for payroll taxes and the federal corporate income tax are added to place cash income on a pre-tax basis

[5] Individuals with negative incomes are excluded from the lowest income quintile but included in the total line

IV. Dynamic Tabulations with the Model

Conventional models can be used to analyze who will benefit in any particular year of the budget period, but cannot be used to analyze who will benefit in more than one year. Treasury's new panel model is capable of capturing the dynamic changes in taxpayers' circumstances and the tax law over the entire budget period, adding the missing time dimension to this type of tax analysis. For example, in any one year of the budget period only taxpayers with children and certain income and income tax characteristics will benefit from the expansion of the child tax credit in EGTRRA. The benefit will depend on the precise year because it drops to its pre-EGTRRA level after 2010. But in each year of the budget period, some currently childless taxpayers will have children and some taxpayers with children will have changes in their income and income tax characteristics, and these taxpayers will benefit from expansion of the credit in years prior to the sunset.

Treasury's new panel model can be used to perform a wide range of analyses that capture the dynamics of both the tax law and individuals' demographic and economic circumstances. The illustration below addresses the question: How many taxpayers will benefit from the provisions in EGTRRA and JGTRRA?

A. Illustration: EGTRRA and JGTRRA

Two sets of simulations illustrate dynamic analysis with the model.[27] The first set addresses the question: How many taxpayers will benefit from the fully phased in level of the provisions of EGTRRA and JGTRRA in the first year and in any year of the budget period? The second set addresses the question: What effect do the phase-ins and sunsets in EGTTRA and JGTRRA, as well as the alternative minimum tax (AMT) have on the number of taxpayers who will benefit from the fully phased in level of the provisions of the legislation over the budget period? The effect of the AMT is included in the second set, even though EGTRRA and JGTRRA contained only temporary provisions affecting the AMT, because the AMT can limit or eliminate the benefit of several provisions of EGTRRA and JGTRRA.[28] All of these simulations cover only non-dependent taxpayers who filed a return in the first year (2004) of the budget period and were alive at the end of the budget period (whether or not they filed a return in any year after 2004).

Certain provisions of EGTRRA and JGTRRA are at fully phased in levels in 2004 and remain fully phased in until they sunset. These provisions include the new 10 percent rate bracket for head of household filers, reductions in tax rates above 15 percent, reduced rates on dividends and capital gains for taxpayers in the regular tax 25 percent and higher brackets, expansion of the child and dependent care tax credit, and EITC simplification. Other provisions are at fully

---

[27] These simulations were performed under 2004 law before enactment of the Working Family Tax Refief Act (WFTRA) of 2004 which extended the capital gains and dividends tax relief from to 2010.

[28] The AMT does not allow personal exemptions, the standard deduction or certain credits, and effectively treats rates below 26 percent as "preferences." Further, the AMT exemption is not indexed for inflation, while regular income tax parameters are indexed. The effect of the broad base and lack of indexing of the AMT will be to reduce or eliminate the benefit of some EGTRRA and JGTRRA provisions for an increasing number of taxpayers over time.

phased in levels in 2004, but then revert to the levels set by the EGTRRA phase-in schedule. These include the new 10 percent bracket (with full bracket widths) for single and joint filers, widening of the 15 percent bracket and expansion of the standard deduction for joint filers, and expansion of the child credit to $1,000. The remaining provisions are not fully phased in (with some not even beginning to phase in) until after 2004. These include the zero rate on dividends and capital gains for taxpayers in the regular tax 10 and 15 percent brackets (effective only in 2008), the repeal of the personal exemption phase-out (PEP) and the limitation on itemized deductions for higher-income taxpayers ("Pease"), and the increase in the EITC phase-out range for joint filers. All provisions sunset at the end of 2010 except the reduced rates on dividends and capital gains, which sunset at the end of 2008 (currently 2010, see footnote 27). The benefit of reduced rates on dividends and capital gains, expansion of the child credit, and the EITC provisions are not limited by the AMT.

B. Simulation 1: Effect of Demographic and Economic Dynamics

The first simulation illustrates the effect of changes in individuals' demographic and economic circumstances on the benefit of tax provisions in EGTRRA and JGTRRA. For this simulation, EGTRRA and JGTRRA law is held constant with all provisions set at their fully-phased-in levels over the entire budget period (i.e., the phase-ins and sunsets do not apply), and the benefit of the provisions is not reduced by the AMT (the AMT is effectively repealed). Tax liability on each return in the panel in each year was first calculated under the law in effect prior to EGTRRA ("pre-EGTRRA" law), but with all provisions fully-phased-in and with the AMT effectively repealed.[29] Tax liability was then recalculated on each return under fully phased in, no sunset, no AMT EGTRRA and JGTRRA law. A taxpayer would benefit from one or more of the provisions of EGTRRA and JGTRRA in a year if their calculated liability under this EGTTRA and JGTRRA law is less than their calculated liability under pre-EGTRRA law. Additional calculations of tax liability for each year were then done to determine whether each specific provision would benefit the taxpayer. In these calculations, tax liability under no sunset, no AMT EGTRRA and JGTRRA law with only one fully-phased-in provision was used. If liability calculated using this law was less than the liability calculated under pre-EGTRRA law, the provision would provide the taxpayer a benefit in that year.

The number of taxpayers who would benefit from the provisions of EGTRRA and JGTRRA was then counted in two ways: the number who would benefit in the first year of the budget period (2004), and the number who would benefit in any year of the budget period (2004-2013). These numbers were then divided by the total number of taxpayers, to give the percentage of taxpayers who would benefit.[30] These percentages are shown in Table 4. Changes in individuals' demographic and economic circumstances over the budget period have a significant effect on the percentage that would benefit from the provisions of EGTRRA and JGTRRA over time. For

---

[29] Effectively repealing the AMT in pre-EGTRRA law is necessary to isolate the effects of EGTRRA and JGTRRA.

[30] In all of these dynamic simulations, the number of taxpayers rather than the number of tax returns is used in the counts because taxpayers can be followed over time but tax return units can change (e.g., when two single taxpayers marry and start filing a joint return). Because the panel follows the same taxpayers over ten years and taxpayers who died during the period have been excluded from these simulations, the total number of taxpayers is the same in all ten years (158.7 million).

example, in the first year 34.7 percent of taxpayers would benefit from the reduction of tax rates above 15 percent, whereas over ten years 60.7 percent would benefit in at least one year. Similarly, in the first year 28.0 percent of taxpayers would benefit from the expansion of the child tax credit, whereas over ten years 41.5 percent would benefit. In the first year, some tax return filers do not benefit from any of the major provisions of EGTRRA because they have no income tax liability under pre-EGTRRA law and do not qualify for the expanded refundability of the child credit. But over time, nearly all taxpayers, 94.4 percent, would benefit.

Table 4
Simulation 1: **EGTRRA and JGTRRA Fully Effective Over the Budget Period, 2004-2013[1]**

Major Provision of EGTRRA or JGTRRA	Percent of Taxpayers Benefiting:		
	In First Year of the Budget Period	In At Least One Year During the Budget Period *(Simulation 1)*	Increase (Percent of taxpayers who gain benefits over time)
New 10% Bracket	78.0%	91.9%	13.8%
Reduction in Rates Above 15%	34.7%	60.7%	26.0%
Reduced Rates on Dividends and Capital Gains	20.9%	42.7%	21.8%
Repeal of PEP and Pease	7.2%	18.4%	11.2%
Marriage Penalty Relief (Except Wider 15% Bracket)	25.5%	49.6%	24.2%
Expansion of Child Tax Credit	28.0%	41.5%	13.4%
Expansion of Child and Dependent Care Tax Credit	4.3%	10.1%	5.8%
EITC Simplification Provisions	0.3%	3.1%	2.7%
Any of the Major Provisions	84.5%	94.4%	9.9%

[1] In Simulation 1 provisions do not phase in over time or sunset, and the alternative minimum tax (AMT) is treated as repealed.

C. Simulation 2: Effect of EGTRRA and JGTRRA Phase-Ins

In this simulation, tax liability for each return for each year of the budget window was first calculated using fully-phased-in, no AMT pre-EGTRRA law, as in Simulation 1. Then, tax liability was calculated for each year using no sunset, no AMT EGTRRA and JGTRRA law, with provisions that were not at fully-phased-in levels (according to the phase-in schedule) set at their pre-EGTRRA law level. In this simulation as in the Simulation 1, there are no sunsets so that the fully-phased-in level of all provisions of EGTRRA and JGTRRA are in effect for 2011 through 2013 (2008 through 2013 for the reduced rates on dividends and capital gains provision). If the first calculation results in a higher tax liability than the second, the taxpayer would benefit from at least one of the fully-phased-in provisions of EGTRRA and JGTRRA. Additional calculations of tax liability for each year were then required to determine the specific major provision or provisions that would benefit the taxpayer.

In this simulation, taxpayers would only benefit from the widening of the 15 percent bracket for joint filers (which also reduces rates above 15 percent) in 2004 and again starting in 2008; full EITC marriage penalty provisions, the widening of the 10 percent bracket for single and joint filers,[31] and the zero rate on dividends and capital gains for taxpayers in the regular tax 10 and 15 percent brackets starting in 2008; the full increase in the standard deduction for joint filers in 2004 and again starting in 2009; the full increase in the child credit to $1,000 in 2004 and again starting in 2010; and the completed phase-out of PEP and Pease starting in 2010.

In Simulation 1 taxpayers could potentially benefit from the fully-phased-in level of all provisions of EGTRRA and JGTRRA in all ten years of the budget period. In this simulation, taxpayers could potentially benefit from some provisions of EGTRRA and JGTRRA for as few as four years. So, the phasing in of some provisions of EGTRRA and JGTRRA reduces the percentage of taxpayers who could benefit in at least one year of the budget period, as shown in Table 5. The reduction in the percentage of taxpayers who would benefit is significant for provisions that phase in slowly, such as marriage penalty relief and expansion of the child credit. In both absolute and relative terms, the greatest percentage reduction is for the repeal of PEP and Pease, the provisions with the slowest phase in.

Table 5
Simulation 2: **Effect of EGTRRA and JGTRRA Phase Ins Over the Budget Period, 2004-2013[1]**

	Percent of Taxpayers Benefiting from Fully Phased In Provision At Least One Year During the Budget Period:		
Major Provision of EGTRRA or JGTRRA	Laws Phased In *(Simulation 2)*	Laws Fully Effective Over the Budget Period *(Simulation 1)*	Reduction (Percent of taxpayers losing full benefits due to phase ins)
New 10% Bracket	91.1%	91.9%	-0.8%
Reduction in Rates Above 15%	58.7%	60.7%	-2.0%
Reduced Rates on Dividends and Capital Gains	39.5%	42.7%	-3.2%
Repeal of PEP and Pease	14.4%	18.4%	-4.0%
Marriage Penalty Relief (Except Wider 15% Bracket)	46.1%	49.6%	-3.5%
Expansion of Child Tax Credit	38.7%	41.5%	-2.8%
Expansion of Child and Dependent Care Tax Credit	10.1%	10.1%	0.0%
EITC Simplification Provisions	3.1%	3.1%	0.0%
Any of the Major Provisions	94.4%	94.4%	0.0%

[1] In Simulation 2 provisions phase in over time as scheduled under current law but do not sunset, and the alternative minimum tax (AMT) is treated as repealed.

D. Simulation 3: Effect of EGTRRA and JGTRRA Sunsets. For this simulation, the calculations of tax liability are the same as for Simulation 2, except that the EGTRRA and JGTRRA sunsets in 2008 and 2010 are in effect for all provisions. Adding the sunset means, for example, that taxpayers could benefit from the full increase in the child credit to $1,000 in only two years (2004 and 2010) and the completed phase-out of PEP and Pease in only one year (2010). The added effect of the sunset on the percentage of taxpayers who would

---

[31] For head of household filers, the 10 percent bracket is always fully phased in. It is also effectively fully phased in any year for single and joint taxpayers with taxable incomes in the 10 percent bracket specified in 2005 law.

benefit is shown in Table 6. The largest effect, as might be expected, is on the reduced rates on dividends and capital gains provision, the only provision that sunsets in 2008. Reductions in rates above 15 percent, marriage penalty relief, and expansion of the child credit are also significantly affected. Repeal of PEP and Pease is affected the most in relative terms.

Table 6

Simulation 3: **Effect of EGTRRA and JGTRRA Sunsets Over the Budget Period, 2004-2013[1]**

Major Provision of EGTRRA or JGTRRA	Percent of Taxpayers Benefiting from Fully Phased In Provision At Least One Year During the Budget Period (with Laws Phased In):		
	Laws Sunset *(Simulation 3)*	Laws Phased In *(Simulation 2)*	Reduction (Percent of taxpayers losing full benefits due to sunsets)
New 10% Bracket	89.7%	91.1%	-1.4%
Reduction in Rates Above 15%	53.1%	58.7%	-5.6%
Reduced Rates on Dividends and Capital Gains	28.1%	39.5%	-11.4%
Repeal of PEP and Pease	9.7%	14.4%	-4.6%
Marriage Penalty Relief (Except Wider 15% Bracket)	40.5%	46.1%	-5.6%
Expansion of Child Tax Credit	35.4%	38.7%	-3.3%
Expansion of Child and Dependent Care Tax Credit	9.8%	10.1%	-0.3%
EITC Simplification Provisions	2.1%	3.1%	-1.0%
Any of the Major Provisions	93.5%	94.4%	-0.9%

[1] In Simulation 3 provisions phase in over time and sunset as scheduled under current law, but the alternative minimum tax (AMT) is treated as repealed.

E. Simulation 4: Effect of the AMT on EGTRRA and JGTRRA Benefits

This simulation recalculates tax liability in the same manner used for Simulation 3, except that the AMT is in effect for the second and subsequent calculations. The added effect of the AMT is shown in Table 7. The largest reductions in the percentage of taxpayers that would benefit are for the rate cut provisions, because some lower rates are effectively "preferences" under the AMT. The percentage of taxpayers who would benefit from repealing PEP and Pease would be reduced by more than half by the AMT.

Table 7

Simulation 4: **Effect of the AMT on EGTRRA and JGTRRA Benefits Over the Budget Period, 2004-2013[1]**

Major Provision of EGTRRA or JGTRRA	Percent of Taxpayers Benefiting from Fully Phased In Provision At Least One Year During the Budget Period (with Laws Phased In and Sunset):		
	AMT in Effect *(Simulation 4)*	AMT Not in Effect *(Simulation 3)*	Reduction (Percent of taxpayers losing full benefits due to the AMT)
New 10% Bracket	87.1%	89.7%	-2.6%
Reduction in Rates Above 15%	50.0%	53.1%	-3.1%
Reduced Rates on Dividends and Capital Gains	28.1%	28.1%	0.0%
Repeal of PEP and Pease	4.6%	9.7%	-5.1%
Marriage Penalty Relief (Except Wider 15% Bracket)	38.6%	40.5%	-1.8%
Expansion of Child Tax Credit	35.4%	35.4%	0.0%
Expansion of Child and Dependent Care Tax Credit	8.7%	9.8%	-1.1%
EITC Simplification Provisions	2.1%	2.1%	0.0%
Any of the Major Provisions	93.5%	93.5%	0.0%

[1] In Simulation 4 provisions phase in over time and sunset as scheduled under current law, and the alternative minimum tax (AMT) is in effect.

F. Combined Effect of Phase-In, Sunset, and AMT on EGTRRA Benefits

The combined effects of the phase-in, the sunset, and the AMT on the percentage of taxpayers who would benefit from the major provisions of EGTRRA and JGTRRA are shown in Table 8. The combined effect of these three dynamic features of current law is fairly significant for some provisions. Nearly 11 percent of all taxpayers who potentially could benefit from the fully-phased-in reduction in tax rates above 15 percent over the budget period would not receive this benefit. Nearly 15 percent of all taxpayers would not benefit from the fully-phased-in reduction in rates on dividends and capital gains, and 11 percent would not receive the full benefit of the marriage penalty provisions. The percentage of taxpayers who would benefit from repeal of PEP and Pease would be reduced by three-fourths.

Table 8

Simulations 1-4 Combined: **Effect of Phase Ins, Sunsets, and the AMT on EGTRRA and JGTRRA Benefits Over the Budget Period, 2004-2013**

Major Provision of EGTRRA or JGTRRA	Percent of Taxpayers Benefiting in Any Year During the Budget Period:		
	Laws Phased In, Sunset, and with the AMT in Effect *(Simulation 4)*	Laws Fully Effective Over the Budget Period *(Simulation 1)*	Reduction (Percent of taxpayers losing full benefits due to the phase ins, sunsets, and the AMT)
New 10% Bracket	87.1%	91.9%	-4.8%
Reduction in Rates Above 15%	50.0%	60.7%	-10.7%
Reduced Rates on Dividends and Capital Gains	28.1%	42.7%	-14.6%
Repeal of PEP and Pease	4.6%	18.4%	-13.8%
Marriage Penalty Relief (Except Wider 15% Bracket)	38.6%	49.6%	-11.0%
Expansion of Child Tax Credit	35.4%	41.5%	-6.0%
Expansion of Child and Dependent Care Tax Credit	8.7%	10.1%	-1.4%
EITC Simplification Provisions	2.1%	3.1%	-1.0%
Any of the Major Provisions	93.5%	94.4%	-0.9%

Notes to Tables 4-8:

(1) The figures in all simulations are based on a representative sample of individual income tax returns filed over the 10-year period 1987 through 1996, and a sample of nonfilers taken from the Panel Survey on Income Dynamics (PSID). The combined samples have been extrapolated to the Budget period, 2004-2013.

(2) The percentages shown for all simulations are based on the projected 2004 population of individuals who: i) are not dependents of another taxpayer in 2004 (or any subsequent year through 2013); ii) file a return in 2004 (but may or may not file in any subsequent year through 2013); and iii) are alive in 2013. Each nondependent individual is counted separately (i.e., each spouse in a joint return unit is counted).

(3) For single and joint filers with income taxed above the 10-percent rate, the 10-percent bracket provision is considered fully phased in only in years when the bracket width is fully phased in.

(4) The reduction in rates on dividends and capital gains is considered fully phased in for taxpayers in the regular tax 10-percent and 15-percent brackets only when their rate on dividends and capital gains is zero.

VI. Conclusions

A. How the Model Improves Tax Analysis

Treasury's new panel model is able to analyze the effect of changes in tax law on individuals over time. It captures the changing demographic and economic circumstances of individuals and the effects of changes in tax law over the entire 10-year budget window, not just a single year. In addition, because it is based on a very large data set the Treasury model is capable of analyzing tax proposals in great detail, more so than multi-year models based on representative taxpayers.

B. Limitations of the Model

Length of time period. The panel model uses ten years of data as opposed to a single year which gives policy makers a better understanding of how policy changes affect taxpayers over time. But ten years is still only a snapshot compared to a taxpayer's lifetime. A twenty year old taxpayer may be lower income than he or she would be at age 30, and he or she might marry, become a joint filer and have children or attend college over the next ten years. Our analyses using the panel model will capture the interaction of these income and demographic changes with proposed tax changes, but it will not capture interactions beyond the first ten years. If the twenty year would not take advantage of proposed changes in retirement savings incentives until he or she were 30, then he or she would not be measured as benefiting from such a proposal in a ten-year analysis. If the analysis were extended to cover the remaining lifetime of such a taxpayer it would give a more complete picture of the lifetime benefits of a proposal.

Ten years is also too short a time period to fully capture lifetime income rankings. Very short term income fluctuations such as one-time capital gains realizations or short periods of unemployment are better measured with a ten year income measure. But separate identification of lifetime poor from "ten-year" poor which may arise from natural lifecycles is only partially achieved. An individual who is 18 at the beginning of the ten year period and in the lowest income quintile may be very different in terms of lifetime income from the individual who is 40 and also ranked in the lowest income quintile on the ten year tables.

Historical basis. The extrapolation approach that the model uses retains the richness of the original data while retargeting certain data fields to reflect the latest data from other sources. Not all fields are targeted, however, and not all trends can be captured. For example, if individuals after 1996 began delaying retirement, divorced in greater numbers, had fewer or more children than they did before 1996, the more recent trends would not be reflected in the model.

Other analyses required for a complete picture. Distributional analyses and dynamic analyses are only two of the tools that should be used to judge tax policies. Distributional analysis by itself only measures one aspect of fairness, vertical equity: the degree to which individuals with greater abilities to pay taxes pay greater amounts. It does not measure the other aspect of fairness, horizontal equity: whether individuals with equal abilities to pay taxes pay equal amounts.

Some other types of analyses used to judge tax policies include discussions of efficiency gains or losses; discussions of simplicity gains or losses; carefully constructed examples of taxpayers affected by particular proposals (e.g. elderly taxpayers, taxpayers with children, small business owners); and counts of winners and loser.

APPENDIX A.1

Basic Data: Constructing the Tax Return Panels

by

James Cilke

and

James R. Nunns

Constructing the Tax Return Panels

The panel model was designed to represent the entire U.S. population in each year of the ten-year period 1987 through 1996. The primary source of data for the panel model came from a panel of tax returns (the "cohort" panel) based on the SOI cross-section sample for 1987. This sample represented most of the U.S. population in 1987, all those individuals who were represented on a tax return as taxpayers (including spouses on joint returns) and taxpayers' dependents. Returns in the 1987 cross-section sample that were filed by taxpayers who were not dependents of another taxpayer were included in the cohort panel sample. The non-dependent taxpayer(s) and any dependents reported on each of these returns were considered a "tax family" headed by the primary taxpayer on the return, and all members of all of these tax families were panel members. Any return filed by any panel member over the succeeding nine years, 1988 through 1996, was identified and included in the cohort panel. Any return filed by a "new" dependent (one reported for the first time after 1987) was also included in the cohort panel. In years after 1987 some non-dependent panel members who remained in the non-dependent U.S. population (i.e., had not become a dependent, died or emigrated) did not file a return, or filed but the return was not identified. All such "missing" returns were imputed by OTA. With these imputed returns, the cohort panel represents over the ten-year panel period all individuals reported on 1987 returns (the 1987 "filing population") and all new dependents (primarily newborns) of this population.

The U.S population that was not reported on 1987 returns (the 1987 "non-filing population") was represented by two additional panels. In both panels, individuals were arranged into tax families following the income tax filing status and dependency rules, and the basic data unit was a (non-dependent) tax return. One of these panels represented the portion of the 1987 non-filing population that remained in the non-filing population in all subsequent years through 1996. This "permanent non-filer" panel was constructed from the PSID. The basic approach was to form tax units from PSID individuals, compute taxable income for the tax unit, and select units with incomes below the filing threshold in every year from 1987 through 1996 for addition to the tax panel. The PSID panel is described in Appendix A.2.

The other ("refreshment") panel was a tax return panel based on the SOI cross-section samples for 1988 through 1996. These samples were designed in such a way that in each year they included a simple random sample of returns with a primary filer who had not filed a tax return in any prior panel year ("new filers"). These new filers included non-dependent taxpayers, and their dependents, who were in the 1987 non-filing population. These new filers also included new non-dependent filers who had been dependents in prior panel years. Since dependents of 1987 filers were panel members and any returns they filed (as dependents or non-dependents) were included in the cohort panel, to avoid double representation of any returns they filed as non-dependents these returns were zero weighted. Non-dependent immigrants to the United States after 1987, and their dependents, were also included in the new filers. Any return filed by any new filer reporting as the primary taxpayer in a subsequent year through 1996 was automatically included in the SOI cross-section samples, so these returns could be identified and included in the refreshment panel.

Whether a return was "missing" in any year of the refreshment panel, and therefore imputed by OTA, depended on the type of new filer. For the first group, 1987 non-dependent non-filers, a missing non-filed return was imputed for 1987 and all subsequent years prior to the first year of filing, and a missing (filed or non-filed) return was imputed for any year thereafter (through 1996) that a return was missing and the taxpayer had not become a dependent, died or emigrated, or had not become a secondary filer.[1] For the second group, 1987 dependents who became non-dependents, it was assumed that any return they had filed as a dependent was already represented in the cohort panel, so no missing return was imputed. In any year after the first year of filing (through 1996), a return (filed or non-filed) was imputed for any year a return was missing and the taxpayer had not become a dependent again, died or emigrated, or had not become a secondary filer. For the third group, post-1987 immigrants, it was assumed that the non-dependent taxpayer filed in their first year in the United States, so no missing returns were imputed for any prior year. If any immigrant taxpayer stopped filing, it was assumed they had emigrated or had become a secondary filer, and no missing return was imputed for years after the last year of filing. A missing (filed or non-filed) return was imputed if there was a gap in filed returns. With these imputed returns, the refreshment panel represents over the ten-year panel period all individuals who were not reported on 1987 returns (the 1987 "non-filing" population) but were reported on a subsequent return by 1996, new non-dependent filers, new immigrants to the United States, and all new dependents (primarily, newborns) of any of these groups.

This Appendix describes how the members of the cohort and refreshment tax return panels were designated, how panel members were followed over time and the tax returns they filed were identified for each panel year, and how "missing" returns of panel members were imputed. Some issues related to panel weights are mentioned, but the full description of weighting is contained in Appendix B.

I. The Cohort Panel

The Statistics of Income (SOI) Division of IRS draws a sample of the individual income tax returns filed each year. The returns filed each year are primarily for the preceding calendar year (e.g., 1987 returns were generally filed in 1988), and SOI samples are normally identified by the calendar (or "tax") year preceding the year the sample is drawn (which is referred to as the "processing" year). Some returns filed each year are for earlier years and some returns cover fiscal (non-calendar) years or periods shorter than a year (part-year returns).[2] There are also some returns filed each year that SOI does not sample: amended returns (because the original returns were sampled) and tentative returns (because the revised return will be sampled).

SOI samples have two basic components, a simple random sample and a stratified probability sample. The simple random sample is based on the last four digits of primary filers' SSNs,

---

[1] Since the "refreshment" panel was selected only on primary filers, when a single taxpayer married and became a secondary filer on a joint return they were no longer included in the panel. However, they were still represented in the panel, as the spouse of a newly-married panel member.

[2] Tax returns must generally be filed on the 15th day of the fourth month following the end of the taxpayer's accounting period (which generally must have a month ending), so SOI samples may include fiscal or part year returns that end as late as August (and possibly even later) of the processing year.

where these digits are from a set of these SSN endings designated by the Social Security Administration and known as the Continuous Work History Sample (CWHS). Since SSN endings are random (or very nearly so) and cannot end in 0000, each CWHS ending represents 1 in 9,999 individuals, making the probability of selection of a return filed by a primary taxpayer with that ending 1/9,999. The stratified portion of the SOI sample selects returns based on the level of income or other return characteristics used to place the returns in strata. Sampling rates vary from the CWHS rate up to 100%. CWHS returns are selected first within each of the strata, with the remaining returns selected randomly, based on a transformation of primary filers' SSNs.[3]

In the latter part of the 1980s, SOI samples were smaller in even-number ("lean") years than in odd-numbered ("fat") years to meet OTA modeling needs.[4] The lean year sample consisted of one CWHS ending (about 10,000 returns) and a stratified probability sample of about 80,000 returns.[5] The fat year sample consisted of the lean year sample plus a second CWHS ending and higher sampling rates (producing approximately another 20,000 returns) in the stratified probability sample.[6] In addition, sample rates for returns with foreign-source income were periodically increased to provide more reliable estimates of such income, increasing the sample by about 6,000 returns.[7]

A. Selection from the 1987 SOI Sample

Most cohort panel members were designated from the returns in the annual cross-section sample drawn by the SOI Division from the 107 million returns filed during 1988, i.e., the "1987" SOI cross-section sample drawn in processing year (PY) 1988. Since (tax year) 1987 was a "fat" year and also a year that covered foreign-source income, the SOI sample drawn in PY88 was about 126,000 returns of the 107 million returns filed. Some of the returns in the PY88 sample were not considered in designating panel members:

---

[3] The transformation creates an 11-digit number that is truncated to a 5-digit pseudo random number (0 to 99999) that corrects for the non-randomness of SSNs. The sample rate for a stratum is achieved by selecting returns with the low-order digits of the transform (taking into account the CWHS selection rate) that represent the sample rate. For example, if the sample rate for a stratum was 2 percent and one CWHS ending was in the CWHS portion of the sample, the non-CWHS portion of the sample in the stratum would be sampled at 1.99 percent (.02 less the CWHS sample rate of .0001 (rounded), less the probability a CWHS ending is transformed to the non-CWHS portion or .02 x .0001, which is negligible), so transforms of 0 through 1989 would be used.

[4] At the time, OTA planned to develop a new individual tax model (ITM) every other year, using the latest fat-year SOI sample.

[5] The lean year sample was referred to as the "Level 1" sample.

[6] The additional sample in fat years was referred to as the "Level 2" sample. The Level 2 sample was identified every year by SOI, but only processed and included in the SOI cross-section file in fat years. Another ("Level 3") sample was identified every year by SOI, but never processed.

[7] Foreign-source income is identified on tax returns by the presence of Form 1116 (Foreign Tax Credit) or Form 2555 (Foreign Earned Income). The over sample of returns with foreign-source income were considered to be part of the Level 1 sample.

- In order to keep the panel at what was thought to be a manageable size, the additional returns selected in the fat year portion of the stratified probability sample were generally excluded.[8]

- The over sample of returns with foreign-source income was likewise excluded.

- Because dependents can only be panel members if they appear on a return filed by a non-dependent taxpayer (including spouses) designated as a panel member, returns filed by dependents were excluded.[9,10]

- Because the panel was designed to represent economic and demographic information on a calendar year (rather than a processing year) basis, prior year returns were not used directly to designate panel members. However, the non-dependent taxpayers (including spouses) and their dependents represented on prior year returns were designated as panel members if they were represented on a 1987 return[11] that was: i) included in the PY88 SOI cross-section sample; ii) included in the 1985-based sales of capital assets (SOCA) panel for PY88; or iii) posted to the Individual Master File (IMF) in any year from PY89 through PY94.[12]

With these exclusions, the remaining returns in the PY88 sample that were used to designate panel members were the 1987 returns filed by non-dependents that had a primary filer with one of the two CWHS endings (approximately 20,000 returns), or that were included in the lean year portion of the stratified probability sample (approximately 70,000 returns). A few of these 90,000 returns, however, were excluded for technical reasons:

- As explained below, returns filed by panel members for years after 1987 had to be identified by panel members' SSNs, which could not be matched if the SSN was misreported on the

---

[8] A few of these non-CWHS Level 2 returns were used to designate panel members because SOI adjusted the achieved non-CWHS portion of the Level 1 sample to correspond to the originally designated targets for each stratum. So, conversely, some Level 1 non-CWHS, non-dependent, 1987 returns were not used to designate panel members.

[9] Returns were identified as having been filed by a dependent if the dependent checked the dependent checkbox on the return or if a Form 8615 ("kiddie tax") was attached to the return. As discussed below, some individuals who were claimed as a dependent on another return filed returns that had neither of the dependent indicators.

[10] Although dependent returns were not used to designate panel members, a small number of the returns filed by dependents that were in the PY88 SOI sample were filed by dependents who were panel members, so these returns were included in the panel.

[11] The 1987 return had to be filed by the primary taxpayer on the prior year return, and only spouses and dependents on the 1987 return were designated as panel members (i.e., spouses and dependents that were reported on the prior year return but not on the 1987 return were not designated as panel members).

[12] So long as the SSN of the primary on the pre-1987 return was correctly reported on that return and the 1987 return, the 1987 return should have been identified by SOI and the primary, spouse, and dependents made panel members. Note, however, that some of the primaries on these pre-1987 returns filed a 1987 return in PY88, but that return was not included in the SOI cross-section sample and, as explained below, no EOYTICK process was run for PY88, so the 1987 return was never identified by SOI and the primary, spouse, and dependents reported on the return never became panel members.

1987 return. The small number of 1987 returns with erroneous primary SSNs were excluded, which meant that no one (primary, spouse, or dependents) reported on these returns were designated as panel members.[13]

- A few amended and tentative returns are unintentionally included in the SOI sample each year because they cannot be identified as such during sampling. A few returns are also sampled that report no income information. These returns remain in the SOI sample, but are effectively excluded because they are given a weight of zero. The amended, tentative, and no income returns included in the PY88 SOI sample were entirely excluded from the panel sample.

- A return with a filing period that ended in 1987 or 1988 was considered to be a "1987" return for purposes of designating panel members. Because of fiscal-year and part-year returns, in a few instances two "1987" returns for same (non-dependent) taxpayer(s) appeared in the sample. Any part year returns were eliminated, and returns ending in 1988 were considered 1988 returns.[14]

In addition to the returns identified in the PY88 sample, late filed returns for 1987 with a CWHS primary that were and identified in the PY89 and later samples were added to the cohort panel by OTA. The identification and other aspects of these returns are discussed in the major section of the paper on the "refreshment" portion of the panel. The imputation of "missing" returns for panel members is discussed in the major section of the paper on imputation of missing returns.

B. Following Panel Members Designated from the 1987 SOI Sample

The panel was intended to include every tax return filed by every panel member for the 1987 through 1996 period. This "following" of panel members required checking the SSNs of all panel members against the SSNs of all tax return filers (including spouses) in every year through 1996. This section explains how this checking was accomplished.

The (non-dependent) primary filers and spouses,[15] and their dependents, reported on the 1987 returns in the 1987 (PY88) SOI sample described above were all designated panel members.[16]

---

[13] Returns with correct primary but erroneous secondary SSNs were retained in the panel.

[14] OTA eliminated the part year returns, and imputed a 1987 return if the taxpayer(s) only had a 1988 return in the PY88 sample. This treatment did not affect panel membership.

[15] Initially, in addition to spouses reported on joint returns, all spouses reported on married filing separate (MFS) returns were designated as panel members. In many cases the SSNs of spouses were not reported or misreported on MFS returns, making it difficult or impossible to follow these spouses. Eventually, it was decided to drop (by zero weighting) all returns of spouses designated on 1987 returns classified as MARS 3 returns (MFS returns which indicated the spouse filed a separate return), but to keep spouses designated on 1987 returns classified as MARS 6 returns (MFS returns on which an exemption was taken for the spouse because the spouse had no income and did not file a separate return).

[16] Non-dependent primaries, spouses, and dependents reported on a pre-1987 (but not a 1987) return included in the TY88 sample were "tentative" panel members until they filed a 1987 return and became panel members, as described above, so were followed as if they were panel members through PY94.

The SSNs of all non-dependent primaries, spouses ("secondaries"), and dependents from these returns were placed on a tickler file. However, the requirement for reporting the SSNs of dependents was new in 1987 and only applied to dependents over the age of four, so many dependents' SSNs were not reported on 1987 returns. Most of these missing dependent SSNs were identified on the 1988 and 1989 returns filed by the non-dependent panel members who (presumably) claimed them in 1987, and also placed on the tickler file.

The SSNs on this tickler file of panel members designated from the PY88 SOI was checked against the SSNs of every primary and secondary filer on every return filed beginning in PY89. This tickler file was created before the beginning of SOI's processing for the year, and was therefore called the "beginning of year tickler" or BOYTICK. Returns identified from BOYTICK were processed by SOI along with, and in the same manner as, returns SOI selected for their cross-section sample for each year. The BOYTICK was updated in 1990 and 1991 to add missing panel member dependents' SSNs, and also updated when panel members' SSNs were corrected (see blow).

After 1987, some panel members filed tax returns with new spouses or reported new dependents. These "visitors" were not designated panel members, but so long as they were reported on the return of a panel member any return they filed was to be included in the panel.[17] To find these returns, each year SOI created an "end of year tickler", or EOYTICK file that contained the SSNs of all spouses and dependents who were not themselves panel members but who were reported on a panel member's return for the year. The EOYTICK file was then checked against the SSNs of all primary and secondary filers on all the returns that had been filed for the year. These EOYTICK returns were then run through SOI's processing system.

The combined BOYTICK and EOYTICK process was designed to capture all returns filed by all panel members for 1988 through 1996 (i.e., through PY97). It would have been necessary to run the EOYTICK process for 1987 (PY88) in order to capture the returns filed be panel dependents that year, but this wasn't done because the design of the panel and the EOYTICK process were not in place by the end of PY88.[18,19] So, nearly all dependents' returns for 1987 were missing from the panel files created by SOI, and had to be imputed by OTA (see below).[20] In addition, because of restrictions on the size of the BOYTICK file, the SSNs of panel member dependents identified in PY89 and PY90 were moved from the BOYTICK to the EOYTICK files for (tax years) 1991, 1992, and 1993. These SSNs were then inadvertently deleted from the EOYTICK

---

[17] The panel was designed to represent "tax families" in each year. A tax family is the (non-dependent) taxpayer, spouse, and dependents, and includes the income (and taxes) of all family members. Since separately filing MFS spouses were eventually dropped from the panel (see footnote 14), only tax returns filed by new dependents were ultimately retained in the panel.

[18] In addition, as noted above, many panel member dependents' SSNs were not reported on 1987 returns.

[19] The EOYTICK process also would have identified any 1987 returns filed by "tentative" panel members who only had a prior-year return included in the PY88 SOI Level 1 sample.

[20] As noted above, a handful of panel dependents' returns for 1987 were selected in the PY88 SOI sample.

file, so most of the returns filed by these dependents for these years[21] were not identified and processed by SOI.[22] For 1993, however, SOI was able to obtain these dependents' return records from the Individual Returns Transactions File (IRTF), which is essentially the input file for SOI processing.

The BOYTICK/EOYTICK process operated only through PY97, so it did not capture any 1988-1996 returns of panel members (or visitors) that were late-filed in PY98 or later years. Some of these late-filed returns were identified by OTA from the PY98 and preliminary PY99 SOI cross-section samples, and added to the tax return panel.

C. SSN Cleanup

Returns filed by panel members and visitors were identified solely through the SSNs contained on the BOYTICK and EOYTICK files. When the SSN of a panel member or visitor was missing or incorrect, any return they filed would be missed in the BOYTICK/EOYTICK process. Further, an incorrect SSN on the BOYTICK or EOYTICK files could match the SSN of an "intruder", someone who was neither a panel member nor a visitor, and the intruder's return could report SSNs of other intruders -- a spouse or dependents -- that would then get added to the BOYTICK or EOYTICK file and could generate additional intruder returns. Any missing or incorrect SSN would make it impossible to link, or would provide an incorrect link, to other records, such as W-2s and the DM-1 file. An incorrect SSN for a spouse or dependent reported in one or more years could also make a tax family appear to have more members than it actually had, and in some instances could affect cross-section weights. Thus, missing and incorrect SSNs could result in both too few and too many returns on the panel file, too many members of a tax family, no or incorrect links to other tax information, and incorrect weighting. Because of the critical importance of SSN cleanup to creation of the tax return panel, SOI and OTA devoted considerable resources to the task.

Missing SSNs. A tax return ordinarily must have a valid primary SSN to post to the Individual Master File (IMF).[23] However, in a very few instances a return with a missing primary SSN was identified for the panel by the secondary's SSN. OTA attempted to fill in these missing primary SSNs in the manner, described below, used to fill in missing secondary SSNs. A primary SSN could also be incorrect (see section below on correcting SSNs), and an SSN reported in the primary position in one year could be omitted from the secondary position on a return for a subsequent year.

At the time the panel returns were being selected, a tax return could have posted to the IMF with a missing secondary SSN. When the secondary SSN was missing on a panel return, SOI would compare the secondary's name on any returns filed for subsequent years with the same primary SSN to determine whether the same secondary was filing with the primary. If the secondary

---

[21] Note that some of these individuals in these years were now filing as nondependents.

[22] Other difficulties in the BOYTICK/EOYTICK process resulted in some of these dependents' returns to be missed in (tax years) 1989 and 1990 as well.

[23] The IMF is IRS's administrative control file for individuals.

appeared not to have changed and the secondary's SSN was reported on one of these returns, it was carried back to the returns with a missing secondary SSN. If the secondary's SSN was not reported on any subsequent return, SOI would assign a unique number to the secondary (or secondaries, if they appeared to have changed) and add the number to the return for each year.[24]

In certain cases, OTA filled in missing secondary SSNs that had not been filled in by SOI. One case is when a joint return was filed in year t-1 and year t+1 with the same primary and secondary SSNs, but only the primary SSN was reported on the joint return for year t. Another case was when a joint return for year t-1 reported both the primary and secondary SSNs, the joint return for year t reported only the primary SSN, and the primary filed a separate return in year t+1. Note that in cases like this if the secondary filed a separate return in year t SOI added the missing secondary SSN to the year t joint return filed by the primary, but the filing status on this return was changed to married filing separate (MARS 3).[25] OTA changed the filing status on such returns back to joint (MARS 2).

Any return on which the number of claimed dependents exceeded the number of reported dependent SSNs was identified as having (one or more) missing dependent SSNs. Missing SSNs for dependents were far more numerous than missing secondary SSNs. As indicated above, 1987 was the first year that dependents' SSNs were required to be reported on tax returns, and the requirement only applied to dependents over the age of four, so the SSNs for many dependents were missing from 1987 returns. Since dependents claimed on (non-dependent) panel members' 1987 returns were also panel members, it was critical for creating the panel to find any missing SSNs for these dependents. To find these missing SSNs, SOI examined the SSNs of dependents reported on the 1988 and 1989 returns filed by the 1987 return primary and secondary, and added back to the 1987 return and to the BOYTICK file the SSNs that appeared to be missing.[26] After these missing SSNs were found and added to BOYTICK, any return filed by these dependents would be identified in SOI processing and added to the panel. SOI did not examine returns filed after 1989 for missing 1987 dependents' SSNs. Further, the EOYTICK file for each year only included the SSNs of visitor (non-panel member) dependents and spouses reported on panel members' returns in the current processing year.[27] So if the SSN of a visitor dependent (e.g., a child born after 1987) was missing for a year and the dependent filed a return, SOI would not be able to identify it and add it to the panel. This was true even if the SSN was subsequently reported and could have been carried back to the earlier years, since SOI did not have the capability of going back to prior year's IRTF records. So, SOI did not attempt to add back missing SSNs of visitor dependents, or of panel dependents who did not file a return.

---

[24] SOI-assigned secondary identifiers were added to about 1,000 returns in panel.

[25] However, SOI did not change the tax computations to correspond to the new filing status, and did not require that the filing status of the year t return filed by the secondary be appropriate (i.e., either head of household (MARS 4) or MFS (MARS 3)).

[26] Subsequently, OTA was able to use date of birth information from the DM-1 file to determine that in a few instances SOI had carried back the wrong dependent's SSN from the 1988 or 1989 return, and substituted the correct one. (SOI apparently did not have access to the DM-1 file when it carried back dependents' SSNs.)

[27] As noted above, certain dependent panel members' SSNs were meant to be moved from the BOYTICK to the EOYTICK file starting in tax year 1991 (PY92), but these SSNs were then inadvertently deleted from the EOYTICK file.

Finally, SOI did not check reported dependent SSNs to see if they were actually the SSN of the primary or secondary taxpayer. As a result, there were more than 50,000 dependent SSNs missing from the panel returns delivered to OTA.

Dependent SSNs are required on returns in order to match each dependent on each return to files such as the DM-1, which provide information about the dependent that is used in OTA's modeling directly, and also to impute missing returns (see blow). OTA therefore attempted to fill in the remaining missing dependent SSNs. OTA first checked all returns with dependents and deleted any reported dependent SSN that was actually the SSN of the primary or secondary taxpayer. The dependent SSNs reported on the last return filed by the primary and secondary were then checked against the DM-1 to determine whether each of the dependents was born before that year; i.e., could have been a dependent in the prior year.[28] These potential prior-year SSNs were then used to fill in any missing SSNs on the prior year return. This process was repeated, moving backward in time through the panel file to the earliest year with a missing dependent SSN.[29] About 35,000 of the missing dependent SSNs were filled in by this process. For the remaining instances of missing dependent SSNs, OTA assigned a unique number, keeping the same number for what appeared to be the same dependent over time.

Incorrect SSNs. There are two sets of circumstances that indicate that an SSN might be incorrect. One is when the SSN is reported on multiple returns for the same tax year and should either have appeared on only one return, or appears inconsistently on two returns. The SSN of any non-dependent primary taxpayer should appear on only one return in a tax year, except for the primary SSN on a MARS 3 or head of household return that also appears as the SSN of the spouse on a MARS 3 return. The SSN of a spouse (secondary) on a joint or a MARS 6 return should also appear only on that one return for a tax year. The SSN of a claimed dependent should not appear as the SSN of a non-dependent primary or secondary taxpayer on a return for the same tax year. Similarly, the SSN of a MARS 3 spouse should not appear on a joint or single return (but can appear on a MARS 3 or head of household return) for the same tax year.

In some cases, the multiple or inconsistent appearance of an SSN was simply the result of an incorrect SSN being reported on one of the returns. In other cases, though, mistakenly or intentionally the same individual filed multiple returns or was reported inconsistently across returns. The main tool for determining whether an incorrect SSN was reported on a return was the age, gender, and name control (the first four letters of an individual's last name (or names, if their last name has changed over time)), from the DM-1 file. If the name control matched the first four letters of the name on only one return and the age and gender were consistent (e.g., spouses had to be at least 16 years old and of opposite gender), the SSN on that return was assumed to be correct and the SSN on the other return incorrect. If the name control matched on

---

[28] There were many instances of dependents apparently being initially claimed in the year prior to their DM-1 year of birth. (This likely occurred when the child was born after the end of the tax year, but before the return was filed.) Absent any other conflicting information, in these instances the SSN was assumed to be correct and could be carried back to the year prior to the DM-1 birth year.

[29] If the "parents" (primary and secondary) filed a joint return in year t, when a dependent SSN was missing, but separate returns in year t+1 (or year t+2 if the year t+1 return was missing) with one of the returns reporting the potentially missing dependent SSN, the SSN was carried back only if the dependent's name control matched one of the parent's in both years.

both returns and the age and gender were consistent, or the comparisons were inconclusive, the individual was assumed to have filed both returns or to have been inconsistently reported on the two returns. OTA retained this multiple or inconsistent reporting in the panel.

When one of a pair of multiple or inconsistently reported SSNs was determined to be incorrect and the (correct) SSN was that of a panel member or visitor, the return with the incorrect SSN could be deleted from the panel (unless a panel member was a spouse on the return). If the incorrect SSN was reported for a panel member or visitor, the SSN was deleted and therefore "missing". The procedures described above were then used to fill in the missing SSN. In addition, since the correct SSN in the pair was that of an "intruder", someone who was neither a panel member nor a visitor, all returns in the panel filed by them, their spouse, or their dependents were deleted from the panel (unless their spouse on a return was a panel member or visitor). About 3,800 intruder returns were deleted from the panel.

A second set of circumstances in which an SSN might be incorrect is when the reported SSN of a spouse or a dependent changes over time. In some cases, the SSN change is simply the result of incorrect reporting of the SSN on the earlier (or later) return(s).[30] In other cases, of course, the SSN changed because the spouse or dependent had changed. To help determine whether the SSN had been incorrectly reported or had actually changed, OTA developed a routine that compared the two SSNs. Each of the nine digits in the two SSNs was compared, and a score of 2 assigned if they were identical; a score of 1 if the digits were not identical, but the digit in one of the SSNs was identical to the preceding or succeeding digit in the other SSN[31] (i.e., a possible transposition error); and a score of 0.5 if the digit in one SSN was a 1 and in the other a 7 or was a 3 in one SSN and an 8 in the other (i.e., a possible transcription error). The possible scores ranged from a high of 18, when the two SSNs were identical, to a low of zero.

The SSN scoring routine was applied to a sample of returns for which the SSN of the spouse had changed. The age, gender, and name control information from the DM-1 file was also used to try to determine whether the SSN was incorrectly reported or the spouse had changed. The results from this sample indicated that the two SSNs were almost certainly for the same individual if the scoring routine gave a score of 15 or higher (i.e., one of the SSNs was incorrectly reported and the spouse had not changed), and that the two SSNs were highly likely to be for two different individuals if the score was below 15 (i.e., the SSNs were different and there had been a change in spouses).

The SSN scoring routine was then applied in all instances in which the SSN of the spouse changed. Based on the results from the sample, if the score was less than 15 the two SSNs were generally assumed to be correct. If the score was 15 or greater, one of the SSNs was assumed to

---

[30] If a return was filed with the same SSN as the incorrectly reported SSN, the returns should have been picked up by the BOYTICK/EOYTICK process and then would appear as a multiple or inconsistent reporting of an SSN (the first set of circumstances). SOI only checked the SSNs of spouses and dependents if another return with that SSN was filed.

[31] If the leading or trailing digit was missing from one of the SSNs there would be 8 transcription errors (which alone would have given a score of 8), but in this case a score of 16 was given.

be incorrect, and the age, gender, and name control information from the DM-1 file was used to determine which of the two SSNs was the correct one.[32]

The SSN scoring routine was also applied in all instances in which the SSN of a dependent appeared to have changed. If the score was under 15 no action was taken. If it was 15 or over the name controls from the DM-1 file of the two dependents and the parent(s) (primary and any secondary) were compared. If only one dependent SSN's name control matched the parent's(s'), it was assumed to be the correct SSN and the other to be incorrect. Any return filed with the incorrect SSN was deleted from the panel. If both or neither dependent SSN's name control matched the parent's(s'), both SSNs were assumed to be the correct.

Other SSN Cleanup Issues. There were several other issues concerning SSNs that OTA dealt with, or examined but did not (or could not) deal with. One issue was the appearance on some returns of more SSNs for dependents than the number of claimed dependents. Typically, this occurred in a year that a dependent was transitioning out of a household (e.g., a child graduating from high school or college and leaving home), or following a divorce. In such cases, OTA tried to determine which dependent SSN should not have been reported and deleted it.

Another issue was the sudden appearance, in some cases for only one year, of a dependent SSN on a return. After filling in missing and correcting incorrect dependent SSNs, it was decided that in most cases there was quite plausible reason for the SSN to suddenly appear: the dependent was a newborn (which could be confirmed from the DM-1), or adopted, or a child whose parents alternated the dependency allowance, or a child who had left home and been independent and now returned as a dependent, or an elderly parent or other relative who became a dependent. OTA had no other information that might have indicated a suddenly appearing dependent SSN was incorrect, so no changes were made in any of these instances.

A third issue was ITINs, which are pseudo SSNs assigned by IRS in instances where an individual does not have a valid SSN. Typically, individuals assigned ITINs are immigrants who are in the process of obtaining an SSN. When these individuals do obtain an SSN and use it for filing, it is not possible to link their returns over time because IRS does not associate their SSN with their ITIN. Therefore, non-dependent panel members with ITINs in 1987 could not be followed once they began to file with an SSN. All OTA could do in these cases was to impute a return for the missing years (see below). In a few cases, OTA was able to replace the ITIN for a dependent with the SSN reported on a subsequent return by comparing the dependent's name across the years.

D. Other Following Issues

Several circumstances made following certain panel members difficult or impossible. Some returns filed by a dependent panel member did not have an associated return filed by the head or spouse of the tax family. This circumstance occurred for several reasons. The head (and any spouse) of the tax family could be panel members who did not file a return for the year because they were not required to file, or filed a return but the return was not identified by SOI because

---

[32] Generally, the spouse had to be over age 15 and within 30 years of the age of the other spouse, to be of opposite gender, and to have a name control that matched the other spouse's.

of missing or incorrect SSNs, or filed a return for the year after the panel was selected.[33] In addition, some dependent panel members changed tax families and typically the head (and any spouse) of the new tax family was not a panel member so their return was not included in the panel. If such dependent panel members did not file a return they were entirely lost from the panel.

A few members of the panel married other panel members or became dependents of other panel members, making them members of two panel tax families. In this circumstance, OTA duplicated the returns filed by these panel members after they switched tax families and associated one of the returns with each of the tax families. The panel member was treated as a "visitor" in the second tax family.

In principle, once a panel member died they were no longer followed in the panel. In a number of cases, however, a panel member who had died (according to the date of death from the DM-1 file) continued to be reported as a spouse or dependent on panel returns. OTA retained this apparent misreporting.

II. The Refreshment Panel

The cohort tax return panel represents over the 1987 through 1996 period the members of the population reported on a tax return filed for 1987, and the new dependents of this population. The refreshment tax return panel represents, over the same period, the members of the population who were first reported on a tax return filed for a year between 1988 and 1996, and new dependents of this population. The refreshment panel represents individuals (nondependent family heads, spouses, and dependents) who were U.S. citizens or residents in 1987 and not reported on a tax return for 1987 but who were reported on a tax return in at least one year between 1988 and 1996; individuals who were not U.S. citizens or residents in 1987 but who subsequently became U.S. citizens or residents and were reported on a tax return between 1988 and 1996; and new dependents of either group. In addition, because of the way it was constructed, the refreshment portion represents dependents in the 1987 filing population once they became nondependents. Since these individuals are also represented in the cohort panel, the dependent members of the cohort panel were given individual weights of zero once they became nondependents. Combined, the cohort and refreshment tax return panels represent all individuals who were citizens or residents of the United States and reported on a tax return at least once between 1987 and 1996, and the filers in each year represent the cross-section of tax returns filed in that year. The remainder of the U.S. population, individuals never represented on a tax return between 1987 and 1996 (the "permanent nonfiling population") was represented by records from the PSID (see Appendix A.2).

The same two primary filer CWHS SSN endings that were included in the PY88 SOI cross-section sample used to designate the cohort portion of the panel were included in the SOI cross-section samples for PY89 and all subsequent years. OTA used this consistency in the SOI sample design to identify the CWHS returns filed after PY88 that were not represented by the cohort portion of the panel designated from the PY88 sample. Returns filed with "new" CWHS

---

[33] SOI's processing of the panel ended in PY97 (although IRTF records for panel members continue to be obtained). OTA checked the PY98 and preliminary PY99 SOI cross-section files for returns of panel members.

SSNs could be identified by comparing the CWHS SSN of the primary filer on the returns against the primary and secondary SSNs reported on all 1987 returns filed in PY88. CWHS primaries on 1987 non-dependent returns filed in PY88 were all designated panel members, so none of their SSNs could be "new". However, since CWHS returns are only designated by the primary SSN, it was possible for there to be a secondary CWHS SSN on a 1987 return filed in PY88 that was not included in the panel but would be represented by the panel. OTA was able to identify these secondary CWHS SSNs from a tickler file that included the primary and secondary SSNs reported on all nondependent returns filed in PY88; these also could not be "new".[34] The remaining, "new" CHWS returns were identified from the non-dependent returns for 1988 through 1996 included in the SOI cross-section files for PY89 through the preliminary file for PY99.

The primaries, secondaries, and dependents reported on late-filed 1987 new CWHS returns were added as members of the cohort panel. Conceptually, individuals reported on these 1987 new CWHS returns represent the non-dependent taxpayers (and their dependents) who filed no return in PY88, but filed a 1987 return in a later year. The portion of the cohort panel drawn from the PY88 SOI sample did not represent such individuals at all, so these late-filed CWHS returns all had a probability of selection of 2 in 9,999 and their weight is the inverse of this selection probability.

The 1988 through 1996 new CWHS returns constitute the refreshment panel. The primaries reported on the earliest new CWHS return filed are members of the refreshment panel; all secondaries and dependents reported on these and later returns are "visitors". Conceptually, refreshment returns should represent the population between 1988 and 1996 who were not represented on 1987 tax returns either because they were in the non-filing population in 1987 or not in the population at all in 1987 (i.e., immigrated), and their new dependents. However, refreshment returns also include the (non-dependent) returns filed by individuals who were dependents in 1987 but who subsequently became non-dependents, a group also represented in the cohort panel. There is no direct way to identify which refreshment returns represent the 1987 nonfiler and post-1987 immigrant populations from the 1987 dependents who become non-dependents. To avoid double counting the last group, OTA zero weighted any dependent in the cohort panel once they filed as a non-dependent. As a consequence of this zero weighting, a secondary on a joint refreshment return could only have a probability of selection in the 1987 population if they filed as a non-dependent for 1987. Rather than check all refreshment secondary SSNs against the tickler of PY88 SSNs, OTA assumed that if the secondary was age 21 or over in 1987 they filed as a non-dependent in 1987, and if they were under age 21 in 1987 they were a dependent (or not in the filing population).

Note that the new CWHS returns were added to the refreshment panel after SOI had completed processing of the cohort panel, so the SSNs of panel members from these returns were never part of the BOYTICK/EOYTICK process, and the CWHS portion of the SOI cross-section sample only follows primaries. So, returns filed by secondaries following a divorce from the primary or

---

[34] This tickler file included a few non-dependent primary CWHS SSNs that were not included in the cohort portion of the panel. Apparently, these individuals filed "no income" returns, which are excluded from the SOI sample. Since filing a "no income" return is essentially equivalent to not filing, OTA left these in the pool for "new" CWHS SSNs.

the death of the primary are generally not in the refreshment panel, nor are any returns filed by dependents. Further, since only primary SSNs are used to designate the CWHS portion of the SOI cross-section sample, if a primary married and reported as the secondary on the subsequent joint return, or a primary switched their SSN reporting position (i.e., became the secondary), the return would generally disappear from the refreshment panel.[35]

III. Imputing Missing Returns

Only under certain circumstances would a return be considered missing, and therefore imputed. These circumstances differed, depending on how the characteristics of the individual included in the panels. This section first describes the circumstances under which a return was considered missing, and then the imputation process.

A. Determining Whether a Return Was Missing

In general, members of the cohort panel should be reported on a return in every year of the panel, and members of the refreshment panel in every year of the panel following their first appearance (in every year of the panel for 1987 nonfilers). If members of each panel were not reported on a return captured in the panel in all these years, in most circumstances a missing return would be imputed. However, there are a number of circumstances in which a member of either panel would not be reported on a return, so no missing return would be imputed. These circumstances differed, depending on the panel and the characteristics of the panel member.

Nondependent Cohort Panel Members. These panel members should be reported on a return in every year of the panel, 1987 through 1996, unless: (i) they died (as determined from the DM-1 file or as reported on their final tax return); (ii) they were believed to have emigrated from the United States (which OTA determined was the case if they stopped filing and their prior return(s) was filed from a foreign address; or (iii) they became a dependent (determined if they began filing as a dependent or were under age 21 and ceased filing; see next paragraph for when a dependent return was determined to be missing). Note that a missing return could have been filed but not captured for the panel,[36] or the panel member could have been a nonfiler in the missing year. The section below on imputation describes how OTA determined whether the panel member was a filer or nonfiler in a missing year.

Dependent Cohort Panel Members. In any year a return for a dependent panel member was not captured in the cohort panel, the return would be considered missing only if OTA determined the dependent actually filed a return; nonfiler returns were never considered missing for dependents and therefore never imputed. OTA calculated the likelihood each dependent without a filed return was a filer using a probit equation estimated using characteristics of dependent filers and

---

[35] Note that such individuals were still represented in the refreshment panel, as new spouses reporting as secondaries, or as new CWHS primaries.

[36] There are several reasons why a filed return by a nondependent (or a dependent) might not have been captured for the cohort panel, including the lack of EOYTICK processing in 1987 and problems with EOYTICK processing in 1991 through 1993; missing or incorrect SSNs, returns that were late filed and not processed through the preliminary PY89 SOI cross-section sample, and errors in return processing. It is also possible that the taxpayer was required to file, but failed to do so.

their parents captured in the TY1995 "family" cross-section sample. The target for the (weighted) number of missing dependent returns in each year was the difference between the number filed that were captured for the panel and the number from the SOI cross-section sample for the year. Targets were computed for ten age groups of dependents. These targets were then hit by setting the appropriate cutoff from the probit equation for each age group. Note that once a cohort panel member who was a dependent in 1987 started to file as a nondependent their returns were zero weighted (to avoid double counting with the new nondependents in the refreshment panel), so none of these nondependent returns was considered missing.

Refreshment Panel Members. Only nondependent primaries were members of the refreshment panel, so in no circumstances was a separate return for a secondary or dependent considered missing. Whether a return was considered missing for a refreshment panel member varied by the portion of the population the member represented: 1987 dependents who became nondependents by 1996; post-1987 immigrants; or nondependent nonfilers in the U.S. population in 1987. As noted above, there was no direct way to determine the portion of the population a refreshment panel member belonged to, but age from the DM-1 file and past earnings from the Social Security earnings file provided indirect information that OTA used to make the determination.

If a refreshment panel member was under age 21 in 1987, they were considered to have been a dependent in 1987 and to have remained a dependent (or non-citizen) until the year they entered the refreshment panel by filing as the primary filer on a nondependent CWHS return. Since returns filed by dependents were represented by the cohort panel, no return for returns for these refreshment panel members was considered missing for any year prior to the year they entered the refreshment panel. After the first year of filing a (filer or nonfiler) return would be considered missing if no return was captured in the refreshment panel for the year and in a subsequent year the panel member filed a (nondependent) return.

Post-1987 immigrants were randomly selected from the returns filed by new refreshment panel members each year who were 21 or over in 1987 and had no recorded earnings in any prior year. The number of returns selected was determined by targets for immigration in the year (which included spouses and dependents).[37] Immigrants were assumed to file a return the year they entered the United States, so no return was considered missing for any year before they entered the refreshment panel. Further, if an immigrant ceased filing, it was assumed that either they had emigrated from the United States, or had remained in the United States but married and began filing as the secondary (effectively changing their status to "visitor"). In neither circumstance would a return for them be considered missing. Only if there was a gap in returns filed, with earnings reflected on the Social Security earnings record, would a (filer or nonfiler) return for an immigrant be considered missing.

New refreshment panel members over age 21 in 1987 who had recorded earnings in a prior year, or who had no recorded earnings and were not randomly selected as immigrants, were considered to have been nondependent nonfilers in 1987. Returns for 1987 through the year prior to the panel member's entry into the refreshment panel were considered missing. If the member was male, he was assumed to have been a single nonfiler in 1987 and in all subsequent

---

[37] These targets were taken from Table 12, "Immigrants Admitted by Age and Sex, Fiscal Year 1986-96" in the 1996 Statistical Yearbook of the Immigration and Naturalization Service.

years prior to the year he entered the refreshment panel. If the member was female, she was assumed to have been a single nonfiler in 1987 but thereafter could have been single or married, and a filer or nonfiler. In addition, after the first year of filing a (filer or nonfiler) return would be considered missing if no return was captured in the refreshment panel for the year and in a subsequent year the panel member filed a return.

B. Imputing Missing Returns

The first step in the imputation process for nondependents who had filed in a previous year was to determine whether the missing return was a filer or a nonfiler return. To make this determination, the filing status in the missing year was assumed to be the same as in the last filed return[38] unless a spouse or dependent(s) on that return filed a return in the missing year that would indicate a change in status. For example, if the individual with a missing return had filed as joint on their last filed return but their spouse filed a separate return (as a single, head of household, or joint with another taxpayer) in the missing year the individual's filing status in the missing year would be set to single (or head of household if they had dependents). The filing status on the missing return and the age of the nondependent taxpayer(s) on the return were then used to compute the filing threshold (the combination of the standard deduction, including the extra deduction for the elderly and personal exemption(s) for the taxpayer(s)) for the missing return. If the filing threshold exceeded the earnings of the nondependent taxpayer(s) shown on the Social Security earnings record(s) by at least $50, the missing return was determined to have been filed; otherwise, it was a nonfiler return.

In the case of 1987 nonfilers, in which the missing returns were nonfiler returns with no preceding filed return, for females the filing status on the first filed return was assumed to apply in all preceding missing years, except that for 1987 the filing status was always assumed to have been single. For males, the filing status in all preceding nonfiling years was assumed to be single, irrespective of the filing status on the first filed return.

For missing nondependent returns that were determined to have been filed, earnings were taken from the Social Security earnings file, with an adjustment if earnings were at the OASDI earnings cap.[39] Earnings were then split between wages and self-employment income based on the split in the last filed return. The implied growth rate in any self-employment income was used to adjust the amount of all active business income[40] on the last filed return to the imputed level on the missing return. All other sources of income and any itemized deductions, as well as the number and type of dependents (absent a change in filing status or a dependent becoming a

---

[38] In the relatively rare cases in which returns for more than two years in a row were missing, the next filed return was used to determine filing status and as the source for other items if it was filed closer in time than the last filed return.

[39] The earnings on the Social Security earnings file available to OTA were capped at the OASDI earnings cap for the year. The adjustment for those over the cap was to assume earnings were the same as on the most recent filed return if earnings were above the cap in that year also, and otherwise to randomly add wages of between 0 percent and 15 percent to the cap.

[40] Active business income includes income from sole proprietors, farm proprietors, active partnership income, and active SBC income.

nondependent), were simply carried over from the last file return. Note that if filing status changed from joint to single or head of household between the last filed and missing return, active business income on the last filed return was split between the spouses in proportion to their self-employment income and that split was used to impute the active business amounts on the missing return, while all unearned income and itemized deductions on the last filed return were split evenly between spouses.

For missing nonfiler returns, which were only imputed for nondependents, earnings were taken from the Social Security earnings file and assumed to be only from wages. Amounts of other income from pensions, unemployment compensation, alimony, interest, and IRA distributions were taken from the last filed return (or first filed return, if there was no preceding filed return), subject to a randomized constraint that kept these sources of income, plus earnings, below the filing threshold. Nontaxable Social Security benefits and tax-exempt interest were assumed not to have changed from the last filed return (except that only half of tax-exempt interest was carried over if the filing status changed from joint to single or head of household).

Missing returns of dependents were imputed through matching of returns with similar characteristics of the dependent and the dependent's parents.

APPENDIX A.2

Basic Data: Data from the PSID

by

James Cilke

and

Janet McCubbin

Data from the PSID

Some members of the U.S. population were never tax-return filers or dependents of filers during the 1987 through 1996 period. Observations from the Panel Survey of Income Dynamics (PSID) are used to represent this permanent non-filer segment of the population. The basic approach was to form tax units from PSID individuals, compute taxable income for the tax unit, and select units with incomes below the filing threshold in every year from 1987 through 1996 for addition to the tax panel. The PSID was also used in combination with Social Security earnings histories and Form 1099 information returns to impute income for years in which tax panel members (who were represented on tax returns for some years during the 1987 – 1996 period) did not file a return, and to impute transfer payments to tax panel members in all years.

The PSID was initiated in 1968. It represents individuals and families residing in the contiguous United States in 1968, and their direct descendants. The initial sample was comprised of 1,872 low-income families in SMSA's and in non-SMSA's in the south with heads under age 60 from the Survey of Economic Opportunity sample, plus 2,930 households from an equal probability sample of households in the contiguous United States. About 18,000 individuals were included in the initially sampled families.

Data for PSID individuals and families associated with interviews conducted beginning in 1988 were used to supplement the panel model.[1] PSID interviews gather income information for the preceding year, and it was assumed that the structure of the PSID family unit at the time of each interview had not changed from the end of the preceding (income) year. Thus, the 1988 PSID interview corresponded to tax year 1987 for the tax return panel, etc. When the panel model was created, final PSID data were available through interview year 1993 (tax year 1992).[2] Over 27,000 individuals are associated with the PSID interviews conducted between 1988 and 1993.

I. PSID Units and Tracking Rules

The PSID definition of a family is a group of individuals living together who are related by blood, marriage, or adoption. In addition, the PSID treats unmarried couples as part of the same family if the cohabitation lasts for more than one interview period.[3] Individuals are classified as PSID family members if they are residing in an interviewed family unit (and are not temporary visitors or roommates) or are members of the family unit but temporarily away and in an institution (such as a school, jail, hospital or the military).

The male member of a couple (married or unmarried) is always designated as the family head unless he is severely disabled. The female member of the couple is designated as the wife if

---

[1] Data for interview year 1987 was also processed, but ultimately used only to assign tax family IDs.

[2] As discussed below, the PSID panel for tax years 1987-1992 was extrapolated to cover the 1993 – 1996 period.

[3] See Survey Research Center (1991), page 13.

married to the head or as the "wife" (in quotes) if not married to the head. In most years, only one member of the family unit (usually the head but sometimes the spouse or cohabitor) was interviewed, and provided information about all of the family members. In general, detailed information is provided about the family head and spouse or cohabitor, and less detailed information is provided about other family members.[4]

All non-institutionalized members of 1968 PSID families are <u>sample members</u>. In addition, persons aged 25 and younger in 1968 who were institutionalized but associated with PSID families (for example, children away at school and members of the military) are designated as sample members. The descendants of the original 1968 sample members are also designated as sample members. Nearly all sample members are followed in subsequent years.[5]

In general, PSID interviews do not cover institutionalized persons age 18 or over. If a sample member age 18 or over moves to an institution (such as a prison, college dormitory, or the military), then the PSID records this fact, tracks the location of the sample member, and attempts to interview the sample member when they leave the institution.

In general, the PSID does not attempt to follow individuals once they become non-respondents. However, beginning with the 1990 wave, the PSID attempts to recontact individuals who had become non-respondents between 1985 and 1989, and who were expected to have achieved age 65 by 1990. In addition, the PSID began to follow non-sample members aged 65 and older if they survived all of the sample members in their PSID family, or if they moved out of the family unit. In the 1993 and 1994 waves, the PSID attempted to recontact a sample of all non-respondents who dropped out of the sample in 1991 or earlier, but who shared a family affiliation with an individual who was still responding to the survey in 1992.

New non-sample members of PSID family units (such as persons who marry or cohabitate with sample members) are interviewed, but (with the exception of some elderly persons, discussed above) non-sample members are not followed if they leave the PSID family.

An important implication of this sample design is that immigrants entering the United States after 1968 (and individuals who resided in Hawaii and Alaska in 1968) are not represented in the core sample. To address this and other issues, the PSID sample design was modified in 1989 and again in 1997. These modifications do not affect our use of the PSID, because we are most concerned with immigration that occurred between 1968 and 1987 (that is, with immigration that

---

[4] Note that if an originally sampled female family head marries (or cohabitates with) a non-sample member, then the sample member female is redesignated a wife (or "wife") and the non-sample member male is designated the head. See Hill (1992), page 40.

[5] See Hill (1992) page 11. Prior to the 1993 wave, sample members under the age of 18 who split off from their family units were not followed unless they set up their own households. Beginning in 1993, the PSID attempts to follow minors who leave their PSID family unit even if they move in with other adults rather than marrying or establishing their own household. When these minors are followed, the PSID attempts to interview an adult in the new household. As a result, it is possible that both the head and the wife/"wife" in the new household will be non-sample members. Prior to 1993, every PSID family has a sample member as the head, wife/"wife" or both.

occurred between the beginning of the PSID and the beginning of the tax panel). Census data suggest that 4 percent of the total U.S. population in 1987 had immigrated since 1968.[6]

II. PSID File Structure and Income Data

PSID data through the 1993 interview consists of: (1) 26 annual family files for 1968 through 1993, (2) one cross-year individual file covering 1968 through 1993, and (3) additional income information for other family unit members (OFUM) collected in 1993.

The family level files include one record for each PSID family interviewed that year. The family file includes all family level information, plus detailed income (for the prior year) and other information about the family head and wife/"wife." The individual file includes one record for each person ever in a PSID family (including non-sample members), and contains individual level demographic and income variables. (There is information for heads and wives/"wives" on both the individual file and the family files; however, the information on the family files is usually more detailed.) The 1993 OFUM file contains more detailed income information about family members who are not the head or wife/"wife."

The annual family files for interview years 1988 through 1993 and the 1993 OFUM file had to be matched to the cross-year individual file to obtain complete information on all individuals for the period. Then a fixed-length individual level file with individual income amounts was created.[7] These individuals were then recombined into tax units, which often differ from PSID family units.

In general, labor income, asset income, AFDC, SSI, other welfare, social security, veteran's pensions, other retirement income, unemployment compensation, worker's compensation, and other transfers are available from the PSID.[8] The creation of individual level income amounts requires imputations for some persons other than the head or wife/"wife". First, until the 1991 interview, labor and asset income was not shown separately for other family unit members (OFUM). In these years, for each person on the individual file the total of labor and asset income is shown, along with an indicator of whether the individual had asset income, labor income, or both. On the family file, total asset income for all OFUM and total labor income for all OFUM are provided. These amounts include only the income earned by the other family members while they were part of the family unit. Asset and labor income of OFUM with only asset or only labor income was assigned, and the total of these amounts subtracted from the family file totals. If there was only one OFUM with both types of income, the amounts of each were the residual OFUM totals. If there was more than one OFUM with both types of income,

---

[6] Beginning with the 1990 interview wave, the PSID includes a supplemental sample of 2,043 Latino households, to increase the representation of Hispanics in the PSID and partially account for the absence of post-1968 immigrants in the PSID. The PSID weights are constructed to allow researchers to use only the core PSID sample, only the Latino sample, or both samples together. Since we are interested in the period beginning with the 1988 wave, we use only the core sample to add non-filers to the model.

[7] Note that some variables are non-missing only for heads and wives/"wives," and some are non-missing only for other persons.

[8] Child support received and help from relatives are also available, but are not used in the panel model.

residual OFUM asset income was divided among them according to the amount their total income while in the PSID unit during the year,[9] or by the amount of time each of them was in the family. (E.g., if each such person was in the unit all year, then the residual OFUM asset income is allocated evenly among them. If one person was in the unit longer, then more of the total asset income was allocated to that person.) Then residual OFUM labor income was allocated to each such person so that the sum of their asset and labor income equaled their total asset plus labor income shown on the individual file.

Prior to the 1993 interview, transfer payments to OFUM (other than social security, which is always identified) must also be assigned to the various types of transfers. This exercise is trivial except when more than one OFUM has more than one type of transfer income. A procedure similar to that described for labor and asset income was used to allocate each individual's non-social security transfer amount across the types of transfers reported for the other family members.

Finally, as noted above, the income amounts reported for OFUM are, in general, "prorated" so that they reflect only the amount earned by other family members while they are residing with the head and wife/"wife". Proration factors which can be used to annualize the income of up to five OFUM are provided on the family file. In addition, the number of months that each person lived in the unit can be determined from data on the individual file. This information is used to obtain annual income amounts for all persons.[10]

III. Creating Tax Units and Taxable Income

The first step in creating tax units was to assign each member of a PSID family unit in each year one of the following statuses: primary taxpayer, secondary taxpayer, dependent child, deceased, away from the family in an institution (e.g. school or a nursing home), and missing.

The first three statuses were assigned using the PSID family head indicator, relationship to family head and marital status. Initially, primary taxpayers consisted of PSID family heads. Secondary taxpayers consisted of persons whose relationship to the family head was wife or husband.[11] Dependent child status was assigned to all other family unit members who were a: child, stepchild, foster-child, grandchild, great grand child, nephew, or niece of the family head or the family head's wife. All other unmarried family members under age 21 were also assumed to be dependent children. Later, the return status of any dependent child who was over 24 years and had income above the filing threshold was changed to return head.

---

[9] For most OFUM, the family file contains a proration factor equal to the fraction of the OFUM's income that was earned while the OFUM was in the PSID unit. If the PSID proration factor was not available, the fraction of time in the family was used.

[10] In most cases, the proration factor calculated from the months data in the individual file is the same as that provided on the family file. It differs when the individual's income was not earned evenly during the year so that the fraction of his or her income earned while he or she was in the unit is not equal to the fraction of the year spent in the unit. PSID proration factors from the family file were used whenever they were available.

[11] As noted above, wives are considered PSID family heads only when the husband is severely disabled, so female family heads are rare.

Female cohabitors (i.e., "wives" of PSID heads) who were PSID sample members were assigned a status of primary taxpayer. Female cohabitors who were non-sample members were assigned the missing status. Similarly, the partners of female cohabitors were assigned the primary taxpayer status if they were PSID sample members and were assigned a status of missing if they were not PSID members.[12]

A status of deceased, away from the family, or missing was easily determined from PSID indicators. All other persons not yet assigned were made into primary taxpayers (or secondary taxpayers if married and female). No tax return units were assigned a status of married filing separately or surviving spouse. An unmarried person with a dependent child was assigned a head of household filing status.

Marital status for the creation of married filing jointly tax returns from primary and secondary taxpayers was determined by the presence of a married-pairs indicator variable. Typically, both spouses in a couple have a married pairs indicator equal to '1'. If there was a second married couple in the house, their pairs value is '2'. The pairs variable together with the interview number is used to link the individual records of married couples.

In general, adjusted gross income (AGI) is the sum of labor income, asset income, pension income, and unemployment compensation. (For simplicity, Social Security income is ignored at this stage.) For married persons, AGI is the sum of these income components for the primary taxpayer and spouse. "Taxable income," defined in the PSID as the sum of labor and asset income, is also available, and in some cases, "taxable income" was inexplicably greater than the sum of labor income, asset income, pension income, and unemployment compensation. Therefore for married couples and PSID heads (except those linked to a female cohabitor), AGI was set to the maximum of "taxable income" for the head and wife or the sum of their labor income, asset income, pension income, and unemployment compensation. When "taxable income" was greater than the sum of labor income, asset income, pension income, and unemployment compensation, the excess was defined as "other" income.

All positive labor income from the PSID is assumed to be wages, all positive asset income is assumed to be interest income, and all positive retirement income (except social security) is assumed to be pension income. If any income source was negative, it was added to "other" income (and removed from the original source). No other dollar values were carried from the PSID to the tax panel file.

A tax family ID variable was created from the PSID interview number. For family heads and spouses, the tax family ID number was equal to the 1987 PSID interview number. If a 1987 PSID child was assigned the status of primary taxpayer in any year, 8000 was added to the interview number. If a second child in the same PSID family was assigned the status of primary taxpayer, 8001 was added to the interview number. Similarly, 16000 (or 16001) was added to

---

[12] Non-PSID sample members have a zero weight, and would have a zero weight when added to the tax panel. Setting such person's status to missing was a simple way of not creating a return for that person, as the return would have a zero weight in any case.

the 1987 interview number of non-child family members assigned the status of primary taxpayer in any year.[13]

Several additional assumptions were made in creating tax units. The number of dependent exemptions on a parent's return was first set equal to the number of "dependent children" in the family unit under age 18 plus the number of "dependent children" age 18 or over with the same tax ID as the parents. In cases where the number of dependent exemptions reported on the PSID was greater than the number of "dependent children" determined by the preceding rules, the following assumptions were made about the "missing" dependent(s). If a "missing" dependent had been imputed in the previous year, it was assumed that the same "missing" dependent appeared in the current year. If one or more dependents was "missing" in 1987, age was imputed using a uniform distribution between 0 and 19. This assumption was repeated in following years (1988 to 1992) if the youngest parent was over age 44, or when there were three or more "missing" dependents. If the youngest parent was under age 45, the "missing" dependent was assumed to be a newborn. In all cases, each imputed "missing" dependent was given a 50 percent chance of being male. All dependents were assumed to be "children at home" dependents.

No tax returns were created for dependents, regardless of their income. However, as in the tax panel, a person who was initially a dependent could become a non-dependent primary or secondary taxpayer.

Individuals who were deceased, missing, or in an institution in all (tax) years 1987 through 1992 were dropped from the file.

IV. Weighting the PSID Units

For 1968, the PSID family weight and the PSID individual weight is simply the inverse probability that the family was selected for the study. In subsequent years, individual weights depend on both the initial probability of selection and non-response adjustments, and the family weight is the average of the individual weights of the sample and non-sample members of the family unit.[14] Non-sample members of PSID families (for example, new spouses or long-term cohabitors of panel members) generally receive a zero PSID weight.[15] New sample members (that is, the children of sample members) receive a PSID weight equal to the average of their

---

[13] If a person's was not interviewed in 1987, the 1987 interview number and all of the other information for 1987 is missing. PSID non-panel members with missing 1987 data were deleted. For the remaining cases, if the 1988 interview number was present, the record was matched to another record with the same 1988 interview number, and the missing tax family identification variable was set equal to the 1987 record number from the matched record. If the 1988 interview number was also missing, the record was assigned a unique number, which serves as a unique identifier.

[14] Non-response adjustments were re-estimated every five years from 1969 through 1989, and in 1993. See Survey Research Center (1998), pages 28-30 for details.

[15] However, as noted above, a supplemental file of cross-section weights in which non-sample members can have positive weights was developed for the 1993 wave.

parent's weights.[16] Thus, for example, the 1993 weights are designed to yield unbiased estimates of individuals and families who are eligible for the 1993 PSID population (i.e., all living individuals who were residents in the contiguous United States in 1968, and their direct descendants).

Note that the individual weight on the file for year t represents both a cross-section and longitudinal weight for persons interviewed in year t. In other words, the weight used to analyze the data for year t is the same weight used to analyze the period (t-k,…t). This is problematic for the analysis of the period (t-k…, t) if an individual responded to the survey in year t and in year t-k, but did not respond in some intervening years. The year t weight will be biased upward because it accounts for the individual's earlier non-response. This is a small problem in 1992 and earlier interviews, because few individuals attrited and then reappeared. The problem becomes larger in 1993 and later interview years, because of efforts to recontact a sample of prior year non-respondents yielded a substantial number of observations with incomplete data. To address this problem, zero longitudinal weights were assigned to reappearing respondents who were non-respondents in the 1988 or 1989 interviews.[17] In other words, sample members who have a non-zero longitudinal weight for 1993 should have interview data for at least 1988 and 1989 (unless they were born to or adopted by a sample member between 1990 and 1993).

The maximal (i.e., last non-zero) individual core sample weight assigned for the 1988 through 1993 interview period is the starting point for purposes of weighting permanent non-filers in the tax panel. This weight is multiplied by 688 to account for the PSID scaling factor.[18] The result is equivalent to the cohort weight for tax panel members. For unmarried persons, the return weight is this new cohort weight for the taxpayer. For joint returns, the return weight is the average of the weights for the primary and secondary taxpayers. No tax return was created if the primary taxpayer (the primary or secondary in the case of a married couple) did not have a non-zero PSID weight.

V. Extrapolating the PSID

When the panel model was built, final PSID data were available only through the 1993 interview year (corresponding to income year 1992). Therefore the PSID panel for tax years 1987 through 1992 was extrapolated to cover the 1993 through 1996 period using a methodology similar to that used to extrapolate the full 1987-1996 tax panel to the budget period. The extrapolation methodology for the full tax panel is discussed in Section III of the paper and in Appendix D.[19]

---

[16] See Survey Research Center (1998), pages 27-28, and Hill (1992) pages 22-23.

[17] See Survey Research Center (1998), pages 25 and 32, for details.

[18] Prior to 1989, the PSID weights were scaled so that they ranged from 1 to 99. (This was done to save space.) The file structure was modified after 1989, and beginning in 1989, weights may take up three digits. However, they are still scaled by the same factor(s) used prior to 1989 (i.e., attrition adjustments have increased the weights so that they are now three digits, but they still do not sum up to the population.)

[19] There are two important differences between the extrapolation of the PSID and the extrapolation of the tax panel. One is that many fewer matching cells could be used in the PSID extrapolation because the PSID sample is significantly smaller than the tax panel sample. The other is that the extrapolated PSID records for 1993 through 1996 were appended to the matching records for 1987 through 1992 to obtain a 10-year set of records, whereas the

To complete the PSID tax population file, returns were created for individuals who were missing in some years, but not deceased. For the years they were missing, individuals were assumed to be single with no income from earnings or investments. It was further assumed that their pension and their Social Security income were both equal to their last observed values.

As missing individuals usually never returned, it is likely that some of them died and their death was not noted in the PSID survey. Therefore, some individuals who were missing for more than two years and who never returned were assumed to have died after their first year of missing. After imputing a return for the missing year, a random number was drawn from the uniform distribution. That number was compared to a value equal to twice their overall probability of dying, given their age and gender. If the random number was less than this value, the person was assumed to die in the following year. Otherwise, the process was repeated for the next year.

After the full tax year 1987 – 1996 file was constructed, PSID panel members who never had income above the filing requirement and were never the dependent of a person with income above the filing requirement were identified. These permanent non-filers were added to the tax panel file.

References

Heeringa, Steven G. and Judith H. Connor (1999), "1997 Panel Study of Income Dynamics – Analysis Weights for Sample Families and Individuals," June 1.

Hill, Martha S. (1992). The Panel Study of Income Dynamics – A Users Guide, Sage Publications, Newbury Park, CA.

Lupton, Joseph, Frank P. Stafford, and Tecla Loup (1999). "Guide to the Family 'Income Plus' Files, Readme, 1994-1997 Family Income and Components Files," March 11.

Survey Research Center, Institute for Social Research, The University of Michigan (1991). "A Panel Study of Income Dynamics: Procedures and Tape Codes – 1998 Interviewing Year, Volume I," Ann Arbor, MI.

Survey Research Center, Institute for Social Research, The University of Michigan (1998). "A Panel Study of Income Dynamics: Procedures and Codebooks – Guide to the 1993 Interviewing Year," Ann Arbor, MI.

Survey Research Center, Institute for Social Research, The University of Michigan (1999). "Panel Study of Income Dynamics 1994, 1995 and 1997 Family Income and Components Codebook," Ann Arbor, MI.

---

tax panel (with appended 10 year PSID sets of records representing permanent nonfilers) was a 10-year sample and was extrapolated as a 10-year block beyond 1996.

APPENDIX A3

Basic Data: Estate Tax Data

by

Deena Ackerman

and

Janet McCubbin

Estate Tax Data

I. Creating the File

Beginning with filing year 1994, SOI has included all 1987-forward individual panel members SSNs in its annual estate tax studies. Prior to 1994, a panel member who died and for whom an estate tax return was filed would be included in the SOI study only if it met the usual estate tax study sampling criteria. Returns transaction file (RTF) data are available for all estate tax returns filed. Thus, limited estate tax data are available for all panel members and more detailed data for many panel members.

SOI and RTF data for filing years 1987 through 2000 were matched to the 1987-forward individual panel. The match yields 6,038 estate tax returns matched to panel members, including members of the refreshment portion of the panel. SOI data are available for 5,338 panel members.

Number of Unweighted Estate Tax Observations Matched to Panel, by Filing Year

Estate Tax Filing Year	With Positive Panel Weights			With Zero Panel Weights			Total
	SOI	RTF	Total	SOI	RTF	Total	Total
1987	11	8	19	0	0	0	19
1988	122	77	199	0	2	2	201
1989	208	122	330	2	2	4	334
1990	328	73	401	1	3	4	405
1991	291	148	439	2	2	4	443
1992	280	127	407	1	3	4	411
1993	332	102	434	5	0	5	439
1994	498	9	507	3	5	8	515
1995	481	0	481	4	1	5	486
1996	490	0	490	5	0	5	495
1997	516	0	516	4	6	10	526
1998	578	0	578	4	5	9	587
1999	528	0	528	6	5	11	539
2000	632	0	632	6	0	6	638
Total	5295	666	5961	43	34	77	6038

The RTF data include most items from the first page of Form 706. This includes taxable estate and subsequent tax calculations. The RTF data do not include the key components of taxable estate: total gross estate and deductions.[1] They also do not include asset detail. The available RTF data appear to be reliable, even though they are not as thoroughly tested and edited as SOI data. Comparisons of RTF and SOI data for a sample of observations indicate that in nearly all cases, the RTF data match the SOI data. Taxable estate on the RTF was inconsistent with that on the SOI file in about 2 percent of tested cases. Estate tax liability after credits on the RTF was inconsistent with the tax on the SOI in less than 3 percent of cases.

Common variable names and definitions have been created for all years of data.

II. Testing the Panel Estate Tax Estimates

The estate tax data matched to the panel and weighted using the individual panel weights indicate that estate tax returns were filed for 633,519 persons represented by panel members who died between 1987 and 1996. In comparison, the SOI data indicate that 617,052 returns were filed for individuals who died from 1987 to 1996. The panel estimate for number of returns is 20 percent lower than the SOI estimate for the 1991 year of death and 38 percent higher for the 1992 year of death.

Overall, the panel estimate for number of returns is about 3 percent higher than the SOI estimate for the ten-year period, the panel estimate of taxable estate is 7 percent higher, and the panel estimate of estate tax after credits is 13 percent higher. If the 1992 year of death is excluded, the panel estimate for number of returns is 1 percent lower than the SOI estimate for the period, the panel estimate for taxable estate is 3 percent higher, and the panel estimate of estate tax after credits is 8 percent higher.

Comparison of Panel and SOI Estate Tax Estimates, 1987 through 1996 years of death
Dollar amounts in thousands

Year of Death	Panel Estimates			SOI Estimates		
	Number of Returns	Taxable Estate	Estate Tax	Number of Returns	Taxable Estate	Estate Tax
1987	44,429	34,913,784	5,462,614	43,996	38,062,852	6,393,717
1988	43,094	47,342,260	10,226,032	45,039	41,692,033	7,432,810
1989	53,106	50,261,948	9,907,185	50,458	48,640,780	8,953,032
1990	56,964	56,842,371	10,097,862	54,328	51,156,471	9,212,028
1991	45,998	52,308,510	10,913,823	57,490	54,102,790	9,626,357
1992	83,093	82,064,297	17,366,500	60,392	57,512,355	10,481,478
1993	77,063	72,550,989	12,145,140	68,991	67,388,010	12,573,827
1994	73,546	66,259,819	11,544,479	71,342	67,707,542	12,321,738
1995	65,043	76,013,483	16,542,043	78,272	76,420,686	14,269,444
1996	91,183	90,389,492	17,795,066	87,330	86,667,116	16,352,185
Total	633,519	628,946,953	122,000,746	617,639	589,350,635	107,616,617

[1] The RTF does include an indicator of the size of gross estate. However, it is fairly crude, and does not appear to have been updated as the filing requirement was increased from $60,000 to $600,000 and the distribution of estates changed. The relevant size classes (i.e., the size classes that virtually all observations fall into) are $500,000 under $1 million, $1 million under $5 million, and $5 million or more. For 1998 tax year, 44 percent of panel members with estate tax returns fell into the lowest class, 51 percent in the middle class, and 5 percent in the highest class.

The discrepancies between the SOI and the panel are to some extent unsurprising. The SOI sample is much larger than the panel sample, and the differences between the SOI and panel estimates may be due to sampling variation, particularly in the panel. The SOI sampling rates for 1987-1996 years of death range from 10 percent to 35 percent of returns per year. The effective tax rates for decedents in the panel averages about 0.7 percent.

The estimates for tax year 1992 are of some concern (the panel estimates are 38 percent higher than the SOI for number of returns, 43 percent higher for taxable estate and 66 percent higher for tax). In addition, the fact that the panel estimates (particularly for number of returns) seem to become more volatile beginning with 1991 might be of some concern.

The estate tax returns of panel members for 1992 do not appear to have been misclassified into the wrong year of death. With few exceptions, the year of death on the individual panel (derived from Social Security records) matches the year of death in the estate tax data (as reported on the return). However, the year of death is missing from the panel data in about 10 percent of cases. The 1992 estimates for average age at death and other factors do not appear very different from that for other years. It does appear that both the unweighted number of returns and the average weight increase sharply for 1992.

APPENDIX B

Weighting the Panel

by

Janet McCubbin

Weighting the Panel

I. Weighting the 1987-Forward Panel

Initial weights for the cohort portion of the 1987-forward panel were derived by Mathematica Policy Research, under contract to the Statistics of Income Division. These weights were modified by OTA and augmented with weights for refreshment portion of the sample. Weights designed to represent the tax filing population for 1987 through 1996 are described in this section. Adjustments to the weights during the extrapolation of the panel to the budget period are described below.

II. Weighting the Cohort Portion of the Panel

The populations represented by the panel include individuals who filed a tax return as a nondependent for tax year 1987, the dependents that they claimed in 1987, the tax returns filed by these two groups of individuals, and the tax families headed up by these two groups of individuals, in 1987 and in subsequent years.[1] There are six different weights on the file delivered to OTA: PWGT, SWGT, RETWGT, FWGT01, FWGT02 and FWGT03.

PWGT is nonzero on returns whose primary filer is a panel member. SWGT is nonzero on returns whose secondary filer is a panel member. Together, PWGT and SWGT for year t sum to the number of members of the panel universe who are filers in year t, including dependents who file their own returns. For a given individual, the nonzero values of PWGT and SWGT do not change. However PWGT is only "turned on" (i.e., nonzero) when that individual files as a primary and SWGT is only turned on when that individual files as a secondary.

RETWGT is nonzero on returns filed by panel members. RETWGT for year t sums to the number of returns filed by members of the panel universe in year t, including those filed by dependents.

FWGT01 is nonzero on one return in each tax family that is headed by a panel member. FWGT01 sums to the number of tax families that have a panel member as a filer (either primary or secondary) on the principal (that is, nondependent) return.

FWGT03 is nonzero on every return filed by dependents who are claimed by panel members (including returns filed by dependents who are not themselves panel members). FWGT03 sums to the number of returns filed by dependents in the FWGT01 families.

FWGT02 is equal to FWGT01+FWGT03, and is nonzero for every return in a tax panel family. FWGT02 sums to the number of returns filed by tax families that have a panel member as a filer on the principal (that is, non-dependent) return. Summing FWGT02 is equal to the number of

---

[1] This is true with one exception: we do not have the 1987 returns of 1987 dependent filers, unless these returns happened to be selected in the 1987 SOI.

returns filed by the sum of FWGT01 tax families. Note that RETWGT, FWGT02 and FWGT03 are all return weights. However, FWGT02 need not be equal to RETWGT.[2]

The derivation of RETWGT, PWGT and SWGT is as follows. In 1987, the probability that a return is selected into the panel is known, and RETWGT for 1987 is the inverse of that probability of selection. The probability that any individual (primary, secondary or dependent) is a panel member is equal to the probability that the nondependent return on which they appeared was selected in 1987. Hence PWGT is equal to the 1987 value of RETWGT in any year that the panel member appears as a primary, and SWGT is equal to the 1987 value of RETWGT in any year that the panel member appears as a secondary.

For years after 1987, PWGT and SWGT do not change (except to "turn on" and "turn off.") However, returns have multiple probabilities of selection, as the original panel member filing units join with other filing units. Consider the following four possible cases for new joint returns: a panel member files jointly with another panel member; a panel member files jointly with a non-panel member who was a 1987 nondependent filer; a panel member files jointly with a non-panel member who was a 1987 dependent (filer or nonfiler); a panel member files jointly with a non-panel member who was not a 1987 filer or dependent. It does not matter whether the panel member is the primary or secondary on the new return. Assume that the panel member is the primary, with probability of selection in 1987 equal to Prob(P). (i.e., Prob(P) = 1/PWGT = 1/RETWGT for 1987.)

In the first case, where the secondary is also a panel member, the secondary's probability of being in the panel, Prob(S), is also known, and is equal to 1/SWGT. Assuming that the probabilities of selection for P and S are independent, the probability that their new joint return is in the panel is therefore 1/[Prob(P)+Prob(S)-Prob(P)Prob(S)].

Next, assume that the secondary was a non-dependent filer in 1987, but is not a panel member. In this case, SWGT is zero, but Prob(S) is known and is not zero. Again the probability that the new joint return is 1/[Prob(P)+Prob(S)-Prob(P)Prob(S)]. Note that even though SWGT is zero and S is not a panel member, her probability of selection contributes to (and reduces) the weight of the new joint return.[3]

Now suppose that the secondary was a dependent filer in 1987. In this case, the fact that S was eligible for selection in 1987 is known, but her selection probability is unknown.[4] Mathematica

---

[2] For example, if a panel member files a dependent return, but is not claimed as a dependent by a panel member, then RETWGT will be nonzero but FWGT02 will be zero. (In other words, if a dependent is not claimed by a panel member filer, then the dependent is not counted as part of a panel tax family, even though the dependent is a panel member.) Conversely, if a non-panel member who is the dependent of a panel member files a return, then RETWGT will be zero but FWGT02 (and FWGT03) will not be zero. It is also possible for RETWGT and FWGT02 to both be nonzero, but different.

[3] Note that the return weight is the same whether the panel member marries another panel member, or whether the panel member marries a non-panel member. In both cases, RETWGT=1/[Prob(P)+Prob(S)-Prob(P)Prob(S)].

[4] Taxpayers should identify themselves as dependent filers if they can be claimed as dependents, even if they are not in fact claimed as dependents (because, e.g., their parents do not file a return). Therefore it is possible that some dependent filers were not eligible for selection. However, the number of such filers is likely to be negligible.

Policy Research (MPR) then "applied the method of multiplicity weighting to calculate RETWGT, setting the weight equal to one-half the sum of PWGT and SWGT (one of which was zero)."

If the secondary was not a dependent filer or nondependent filer in 1987, but was under age 21 at the end of 1987, then MPR assumes that the secondary was eligible to be selected as a dependent in 1987. Then as in the preceding case, the return weight is half of PWGT.

Finally, if the secondary was not a dependent or nondependent filer in 1987 and was age 21 or over at the end of 1987, then MPR assumes that the secondary was not in the 1987 filing population. In this case, Prob(S) is 0, and the return weight is 1/[Prob(P)].

Assuming that all non-filers under age 21 were dependents in 1987 overstates the number of dependent children; and assuming that all non-filers over age 21 were not dependents in 1987 understates the number of dependent adults. MPR asserts that by choosing 21 as the cutoff, the errors are, on average, approximately offsetting.

In order to determine weights for joint returns in the panel with new non-panel member spouses after 1993, the probability of selection for the new person (i.e., Prob(S) in the above cases) is assumed to be equal to the individual's CWHS probability of selection. To the extent that some of the new persons were not eligible for selection in 1987, this will overstate the probabilities of selection and understate the return.

III. Weighting the Post-1987 Entrants to the Filing Population

The panel does not represent individuals who were not filers or claimed dependents in 1987. New individuals include nondependent primaries in 1988 or later who were not filers or dependents in 1987; nondependent secondaries in 1988 or later who were not filers or dependents in 1987; dependents in 1988 or later who were not filers or dependents in 1987. (It may also include persons represented on tax year 1987 returns that were filed very late.) To represent these new individuals, CWHS returns of primaries who were not primaries or secondaries in 1987 were added to the panel. Some of these individuals were dependents in 1987. Therefore to avoid overrepresenting persons who were dependents in 1987, weights of zero are assigned to returns of panel members who were dependents in 1987 as they become non-dependent filers. The CWHS returns represent all new nondependent filers.

The probability of selecting a new return in any year after 1987 is equal to the CWHS probability of selecting the primary, Prob(P). The individual weights for the primary and secondary and the return weight are all 1/Prob(P).

Note that the CWHS returns do not represent a true panel. Therefore the probability that a return is selected to refresh the panel in 1989 is not contingent on whether any of the individuals on the return were selected in 1988. The probability of selection in 1989 is contingent only on whether the primary or secondary were filers in 1987, and on the primary's SSN. This makes the weighting very easy, but it creates problems for analysis. If a secondary divorces the primary and is not selected based on her own SSN (or based on the primary SSN of a new joint return), then she is lost from the panel. Similarly, if a CWHS primary becomes a secondary and his spouse is not selected, then the primary is lost from the panel. (This would occur if the primary and secondary continue to file jointly, but switch positions on the return.)

References

Czajka, John. (1999). "Responses to David's Responses, September 23, 1999."

Westat (1999). "Meeting Minutes, September 24, 1999."

APPENDIX C.1

Imputations: Consumption

by

James Cilke

and

Julie-Anne Cronin

Consumption

I. Introduction

A measure of each family's relative consumption of taxed goods is needed to distribute excise taxes. The tax data used by Treasury's Office of Tax Analysis (OTA) to develop its panel model does not include information on consumption. This paper describes the methodology used to impute consumption to panel members.

We had three goals in mind when trying to impute consumption. First, to accurately reflect total consumption by category of good for all families and across income classes. Second, to provide reasonable variation in consumption within and across socio-economic classes. Third, to maintain realistic cross-correlations among broad categories of consumption.

There were a number of strategies we could have used to impute consumption. We could have attempted to estimate a system of demand equations, the sum of which would have been equal to total consumption. Such a system, if well-constructed, would preserve cross correlations among types of goods within a family. Unfortunately the price and quantity information needed to estimate such a system was not available.

Alternatively, we could have used regression analysis to measure expenditures on particular goods as a function of the income and demographic information available in both the consumption and tax data. Such a methodology would not, however, have maintained cross correlations across goods. Variation in consumption patterns would also have been limited to known regressors.

To maintain cross correlations as well as variation in the consumption data, we chose to perform an unconstrained match between the Consumer Expenditure Survey (CEX) and the tax data. Because the match was unconstrained (some families were matched repeatedly and others in the consumption data were not used) the imputed consumption on the panel does not have the same level of variation as the consumption data but more so than if we had used a regression technique.

Below we discuss i) the consumption data; ii) the matching methodology; iii) the separate imputation for cigarette consumption; and iv) some results from the match.

II. The Consumer Expenditure Survey

A. Design

We imputed shares of consumption from the CEX. It is designed to represent the civilian non-institutionalized population. In the CEX, the unit of analysis is the "consumer unit" (CU), defined as one of the following: i) all related members of a household; ii) a person living alone or in a group but who is financially independent; or iii) two or more persons living together who use their joint income to make joint expenditures.

The CEX data is collected in quarters. Each quarter is nationally representative and includes approximately 5,000 CUs. The sample for each quarter is divided in three (each nationally representative) so that only one-third of the quarter sample is interviewed in the first month of the quarter, one third in the second month of the quarter, and one-third in the last month of the quarter. The CUs are questioned about the previous three months consumption (e.g. a CU in the first quarter of 1995 that is interviewed in January will provide consumption information from October through December of 1994).

The CEX has a rotating panel nature. Each selected CU is interviewed for 5 quarters. The first quarter is not recorded. In any given quarter, approximately 20 percent of the CUs interviewed will be in their first interview, 20 percent in their second interview, 20 percent in their third interview, etc.

B. Limitations

Although the CEX provided the most detailed consumption information available, it did have some severe limitations. As mentioned above, it lacked price and quantity information, making it difficult to use the data to create a system of demand equations. It also suffered from poor income data, attrition bias, and underreporting of key consumption categories.

Transfer and capital income, in particular, were underreported in the CEX; making it especially difficult to measure the consumption to income ratios for the bottom and top ends of the income distribution. As a result, we did not use income as a matching variable. Instead we derived an annual consumption measure in the tax data and matched families in the two data sets by annual consumption. Our proxy for consumption in the tax data was positive after-tax cash income.[1]

Each quarter of the CEX was nationally representative. We chose two quarters (the first quarter of 1995 and the first quarter of 1996) and followed the families represented in these quarters forward and backward to get a full year of consumption.[2] We used two quarters, as opposed to one in order to increase the size of the CEX sample. Because consumption for any given family was only collected for four quarters, the two samples did not overlap.

Many families, however, were missing one of the four interviews that made up a year's consumption. The missing interviews were imputed by substituting the consumption of a similar family in the same interview quarter. Special care was taken with families in their final interview since the final interview included consumption items not recorded in previous interviews.

---

[1] Cash income excludes many forms of savings such as employee and employer contributions to defined benefit and defined contribution pension plans, inside build-up on defined contribution pension plans, accrued (but not realized) capital gains (including personal residences), and inside build-up on other tax-preferrred savings accounts (IRAs, 529s etc.).

[2] For example, if a family was in its final interview in the first quarter of 1995, we picked up that family's consumption from the second, third and fourth quarters of 1994 to create an annual consumption measure. All consumption amounts were indexed to the first quarter of 1996 by the CPI-U.

The CEX, like many surveys, underreported alcohol, gasoline, and cigarette consumption. Because the reporting of cigarette consumption was particularly poor, we separately imputed cigarette usage using information from the National Institute of Health Survey (NIHS). Section IV below describes this imputation.

C. File Preparation

The Bureau of Labor Statistics organized the CEX data for each interview quarter into 4 files: the family file, MTAB, ITAB, and the diary file. The family file contained aggregated consumption data as well as general demographic information. The MTAB file contained detailed expenditure information for each universal classification code (UCC) for each month of each interview quarter. The ITAB file contained detailed income information for each month of the interview quarter. The diary file contained monthly expenditures on certain minor expenditures. The CEX data for our consumption imputation was drawn primarily from the family file and was supplemented by the MTAB and ITAB files. The diary file was not used.

We imputed 15 broad categories of expenditures as well as three subcategories of expenditures subject to excise. The aggregate expenditure data were drawn from the family file and included expenditures on food, alcoholic beverages, housing, apparel, transportation, health, entertainment, personal care, reading, education, tobacco, miscellaneous items, charitable contributions, and pensions and life insurance. We also collected demographic information that was used in the match: the number of adults and number of children in the family, and the gender, age, and marital status of the family head.

Because the broad categories of expenditures included durable goods, they had to be adjusted before they could be used to create annual consumption measures.[3] Durable goods are consumed over time so expenditures on durable goods in a given year do not accurately reflect consumption of the durable in that year. Ideally expenditures on a car, for example, would be spread over the car's usable lifetime. Unfortunately, with only four quarters of consumption data, it was not possible to know which families were currently "consuming" previously purchased durable goods.

Our next best alternative was to exclude the purchases of durable goods from our measure of consumption.[4] Using the definition of durable goods found in the National Income and Product Accounts (NIPA Table 2.4) and the MTAB file, we created a nondurable good measure for each consumption category. Table 1 lists the durable goods in each expenditure category and shows their relative magnitude.

---

[3] They did not, however, include housing purchases which, along with principal repayments, are considered a form of savings not consumption.
[4] Although we matched on nondurable expenditures, we imputed both durable and nondurable expenditures.

Table 1: Description and Amount of Durable Goods				
Aggregate Consumption Category		Durables		Non-Durables
Description	$B	Description	$B	$B
Food	548	No durables	0	548
Alcoholic beverages	36	No durables	0	36
Housing	1,056	Furntiture, appliances, and computers	101	952
Apparel	160	Jewelry and watches	15	146
Transportation	663	New and used motor vehicles, tires, tubes and other parts	353	312
Health	120	Orthopedic and opthalmic products and appliances	8	114
Entertainment	156	Recreation and sports equipment	56	100
Personal care	28	No durables	0	28
Reading	15	Books and maps	5	11
Education	37	Books and maps	4	32
Tobacco	23	No durables	0	23
Miscellaneous	67	No durables	0	67
Charitable contributions	98	No durables	0	98
Pensions and life insurance	264	No durables	0	264
Total	3,270		541	2,730

We also used the MTAB file to collect amounts for the consumption of gasoline, air travel and telephone services. These expenditures were relatively narrow in scope and were not separately identified in the family file but are subject to excise taxes.

The ITAB was used to adjust the miscellaneous expenditures only collected in the final interview.[5] Because these amounts were only collected for one-fourth of the sample (those families in the final interview), they were multiplied by 4 during BLS processing, so that the sum of expenditures in this category represented the population total. Because we were annualizing the data, we had a final interview for each family and, therefore, needed to "undo" the BLS adjustment to these expenditures by dividing them by 4.

III. Matching the CEX to the Tax Data

To impute consumption to the panel model, we performed an unconstrained statistical match between tax families on the panel and families from the CEX. The CEX file consisted of approximately 7,600 families with levels of total annual consumption expenditures (at 1996 levels), including expenditures on 20 additional specific items. Many of these items are subject to, or are strongly related to Federal excise taxes.

Our **a priori** notion was that a family's consumption pattern would remain fairly constant over time and that significant changes in consumption patterns would occur only when a family experienced a major change in membership or income. The basic strategy was to first match base year 1987 tax families to the consumption file. If the family was stable in subsequent years, then consumption shares of each item would remain the same for those years. Alternatively, families that experienced a major change would be rematched to a new CEX record.

---

[5] The ITAB file primarily contains income, not expenditure data. The "income" item included as part of the miscellaneous expenditures are "employee business expenses."

In total, we used seven matching variables. The first, Family Status Class, contained four possible values: non-married without children, non-married with children, married without children, and married with children. The marital status refers to the head of the family. A child was defined as a person under the age of 18. The child status referred to the entire family. The existence of any child living with the family, independent of its relationship to the head of the family, resulted in the designation "with children." The Family Status variable was required to match exactly.

The second matching variable was the age of the primary taxpayer, which matches to the age of the family head on the CEX file. For non-married families, the gender of the family head was the third matching variable. The fourth matching variable was the number of children in the family. In the tax records, this variable was defined as the number of dependents aged 17 and under.

The fifth matching variable was the number of "extra" adults in the family, persons age 18 and over excluding the family head and spouse (if married). In the tax records, this variable was defined as dependents age 18 and over. Because CEX families were not tax families, some family members in the CEX were not claimed as a dependent by the family head. As a result, the number of children and "extra" adults in the CEX file was sometimes larger than in the tax file. For this reason, the penalties for mis-matches on the number of children and the number of extra adults was relatively small.

The sixth matching variable was a consumption ranking variable. On the tax panel, consumption was proxied by total positive income after-tax. Total positive income was the sum of the positive income items included in AGI, including all Social Security benefits, tax exempt interest, and the foreign earned income exclusion. From this, Federal income taxes and own FICA and SECA taxes were subtracted.[6]

Tax families were then ranked by centile. For example, the median family had a rank of 50 and the top 1 percent of families had a rank of 100. Since the lowest 7 or 8 percent of families had zero positive after-tax income, we decided to collapse the first 10 ranks into a single value of 1 and subtracted 10 points from each persons rank over 11. The resulting income ranks range from 1 to 90.

We created a similar ranking variable on the CEX file, except that families were ranked by their total consumption. Again, the values of this variable ranged from 1 to 90. Table 2 below summarizes the matching variables and the penalty assigned to a mis-match. The actual matching CEX record to a particular tax record was the one with the lowest calculated penalty. A single CEX record was matched multiple times.

---

[6] Ideally, we would have liked to subtract all personal taxes, including health insurance, estate taxes, and state and local income taxes. Unfortunately, these additional taxes were not available in the tax data prior to the consumption imputation.

Table 2: Mis-Matching Penalties

Matching Variable	Penalty
Family Status Class	Infinite
Age of Primary	200 points
Gender (for non-joints)	500 points
Number of children in the family[1]	75 points per person
Number of extra adults[2]	75 points per person
Consumption Rank[3]	100 points per centile
Smoking status	1000 points

[1] Children are defined as persons age 17 and under

[2] Extra adults are defined as persons age 18 and older, not including the head of household (primary) or spouse.

[3] In the tax data, consumption is defned as total positive income, after-tax.

The only CEX information brought over to the tax file were the expenditure shares (expenditures on item x divided by total expenditures). On the panel model, total consumption by the tax family was proxied by positive after-tax cash income. The values for the 20 individual consumption items are created by multiplying the imputed shares from the CEX by total consumption on the panel to arrive at the separate consumption categories.

If, in the next year, the tax family remained stable, then total consumption for the family was the previous year's total consumption adjusted by the percentage change in the family's total positive after-tax income.[7] So, for example, if a family's positive after-tax income rose by five percent then total consumption also rose by five percent.

If a tax family was not stable, then a new match to the CEX was performed. Families were considered unstable if: 1)The family status variable changed (e.g. an unmarried person married or a couple had a child); 2) The family's income rank changed by more than 10 points relative to the original matching year; or 3) The family's smoking status changed.

IV. Tobacco Imputation

We imputed the consumption of tobacco to individuals not families. Unlike most other goods, tobacco was not universally consumed. It is also habit forming but only at the individual level. Whether or not a family was designated as "smoking" depended on its membership. As family membership changed over time so did the smoking status of the family.

---

[7] The percentage change in income is capped at plus or minus 25 percent.

A. Imputing Smoking Status.

The first step to imputing a smoking status to each individual on the tax file was to randomly assign each individual in the tax file a "Smoking Selection Cutoff" number. It was simply a random, uniformly distributed number between zero and one. Once assigned, the number never changed.

Next, using data from the National Institute of Health Survey (NIHS), we constructed a table of smoking probabilities by family income class, age class, and marital status for all adults (see Table 3). The table included a total of 60 cells. As shown in the table, unmarried persons in the lowest income class and in the 34-45 age class had the highest probability of smoking (46 percent). The lowest probability of smoking (2 percent) was associated with married persons in the highest income class, over 65 years of age.

Table 3: Percent of Adults Who Smoke by Income, Age, and Marital Status

Family Income	Age						
	18 to 24	25 to 34	35 to 44	45 to 54	55 to 64	65 & over	All ages
--- All adults ---							
$0 to $20,000	30	34	43	40	31	12	29
$20,000 to $30,000	35	30	39	35	29	9	29
$35,000 to $55,000	25	25	30	27	23	9	25
$55,000 to $75,000	20	22	27	21	19	9	22
over $75,000	23	16	15	15	12	4	15
All Incomes	27	25	29	25	22	10	24
--- Married ---							
$0 to $20,000	21	29	39	33	26	11	25
$20,000 to $30,000	34	27	33	35	27	8	25
$35,000 to $55,000	19	23	28	25	23	8	23
$55,000 to $75,000	20	19	25	21	16	8	20
over $75,000	*	12	14	14	13	2	13
All Incomes	25	21	24	21	19	8	20
--- Single ---							
$0 to $20,000	31	36	46	46	34	13	31
$20,000 to $30,000	36	33	44	35	32	13	33
$35,000 to $55,000	27	30	32	30	22	10	28
$55,000 to $75,000	20	29	36	21	36	13	26
over $75,000	22	26	23	27	11	9	22
All Incomes	28	32	39	34	30	13	29

Source: National Institute of Health Survey, 2000.

* fewer than 40 observations

Table 4 shows the overall percent distribution of the adult population within each of the NIHS' income classes. For example, 25.3 percent of the adult population fell in the lowest income class, 23.5 percent in the next income class, and so on. In the tax data, we calculated the dollar breaks in each year (1987 to 1996) using the panel model's family cash equivalent income measure so that the percent of the adult population in each class matched the distribution in Table 3.

The next step was to impute smoking status to each adult person in each year.[8] This was accomplished by simply comparing each adult person's Smoking Selection Cutoff number with the appropriate probability of smoking given the person's income, age and marital status. If the selection number was less than the probability number, the person was a smoker in that year.[9]

Table 4: Distribution of NHIS Families by Income Class	
Family Income Class	Percent Distribution
$0 to $20,000	25.3
$20,000 to $35,000	23.5
$35,000 to $55,000	21.9
$55,000 to $75,000	14.0
over $75,000	15.3
All Incomes	100.0

Table 3 only applied to the adult population. Additional information from the NIHS suggested that more than half of all smokers began smoking before age 18. As a result, we decided to extend the imputation to dependents between the inclusive ages of 13 and 17. The selection probabilities for the youngest age classes were adjusted by the following amounts: 0.18 for 13 year olds, 0.28 for 14 year olds, 0.44 for 15 year olds, 0.64 for 16 year olds, and 0.79 for 17 year olds.

The final output from the imputation routine were two arrays. The first showed for each person, the years in which he or she smoked. The second showed for each non-dependent return, the number of smokers on the return for that year. The imputation process captured the notion that people tend to smoke year after year. The process almost assures that a person in year t who was in the same income, age, and marital status class in year t+1 would have the same smoking status. However, the imputation process did not capture any smoking relationships among family members. Each person was treated independently. So for example, in our imputation smokers were not more likely to be married to another smoker, and children of smokers were not more likely to smoke.

V. Some Results from the Imputation

---

[8] For our purposes, adults are all independent filers and nonfilers regardless of age and all dependents age 18 or over.

[9] The age and marital status distributions on the panel model are slightly different from those in Table 2. The end result is that slightly too many people are assigned a smoking status. To correct this, we increased each person's Smoking Selection Cutoff value by 0.012.

Tables 5a-5d show the distribution of total consumption by category across quintiles of nondurable consumption. Tables 6a-6d show the distribution of total consumption by quintile of nondurable consumption across consumption categories. Tables 7a-7d show the same distributions for excise goods. All tables labeled "a" refer to distributions for the four quarters of expenses for all families interviewed for the CEX in the first quarter of 1994; "b" tables refer to expenses for families interviewed in the first quarter of 1995; "c" tables refer to the first year of the imputation (1987); and "d" tables refer to the last year of the imputation (1996).

In general, and as shown in tables 6a-6d, the distributions for the imputed panel years ("c" and "d" tables) are very similar to the distributions found in the annualized CEX data ("a" and "b" tables). Only the distributions of health and education expenditures show relatively minor differences. The CEX shows slightly more health and less education expenditures for families with less overall consumption than the imputations for 1987 and 1996.

Total education expenditures, although they may be a large component of a family's budget in a particular year, are relatively small in size as a percent of total expenditures for all families, only 1 percent (see Tables 7a-7d). Tuition expenses which are crucial to the measurement of tuition tax credits are being separately imputed (see Appendix C2 for more detail).

The health expenditure in this imputation is of limited value. Health expenditures in the CEX only include out-of-pocket expenses. Expenses reimbursed by health insurers are not included. In fact, out-of-pocket expenses may be negative when a family is reimbursed in the current year for expenses incurred in a prior year.

Because the consumption of health services is a major component of overall consumption and the center of many tax policy decisions, the value of employee provided health insurance, was separately imputed (see Appendix C3 for more detail).

Although the distributions of consumption in the CEX and the imputation are very similar, the levels of consumption imputed to the panel model are about 50 percent higher than in the CEX for all goods except tobacco. Consumption on the panel model is generally much greater than in the CEX. Because we only impute consumption shares, not total consumption, from the CEX, we maintain the panel model's greater level of total consumption in the imputation.

Table 5a: Four Quarters of Expenses for CU's Present in 1994(1)-- Percent Distribution Across Expenditure Quintile

(1987 Expenditure Levels)

Quintile of Nondurable Consumption	Total	Food	Alchohol	Housing	Apparel	Transport	Health	Entertainment	Personal Care	Reading	Education	Tobacco	Misc - all qtr	Misc- 5th qtr	Contrib.	Pensions and Life Insurance
--- All Goods ---																
Lowest	7	9	7	8	5	5	10	5	8	7	5	10	4	6	4	2
2nd	12	14	12	12	10	12	13	9	13	11	7	19	10	11	8	7
3rd	17	17	17	16	15	19	19	15	17	18	11	22	15	18	16	14
4th	24	24	24	24	25	25	23	25	26	26	18	26	24	26	20	25
Highest	41	35	41	40	46	38	35	46	37	38	60	23	48	38	51	52
Total	100	100	100	100	100	100	100	100	100	100	100	100	100	100	100	100
--- Nondurable Goods ---																
Lowest	7	9	7	8	5	5	10	5	8	8	3	10	4	6	4	2
2nd	12	14	12	12	10	11	14	9	13	13	6	19	10	11	8	7
3rd	16	17	17	16	15	17	19	14	17	18	10	22	15	18	16	14
4th	24	24	24	24	25	25	23	25	26	26	18	26	24	26	20	25
Highest	41	35	41	40	44	42	35	48	37	35	63	23	48	38	51	52
Total	100	100	100	100	100	100	100	100	100	100	100	100	100	100	100	100
--- Durable Goods ---																
Lowest	6			7	3	6	8	5		5	17					
2nd	12			12	8	12	12	8		8	12					
3rd	19			15	13	21	20	17		17	13					
4th	25			24	20	25	26	25		26	19					
Highest	38			42	57	36	35	44		44	39					
Total	100			100	100	100	100	100		100	100					

Table 5b: Four Quarters of Expenses for CU's Present in 1995(1)-- Percent Distribution Across Expenditure Quintile

(1987 Expenditure Levels)

--- All Goods ---

Quintile of Nondurable Consumption	Total	Food	Alchohol	Housing	Apparel	Transport	Health	Entertainment	Personal Care	Reading	Education	Tobacco	Misc - all qtr	Misc - 5th qtr	Contrib.	Pensions and Life Insurance
Lowest	7	10	7	8	5	5	10	5	8	7	5	13	4	4	5	2
2nd	12	15	14	13	11	12	15	11	13	13	7	19	10	12	10	7
3rd	18	19	17	17	17	22	20	16	19	18	11	22	14	24	14	16
4th	23	22	22	22	24	25	22	23	23	24	19	25	21	25	24	26
Highest	39	34	40	40	44	37	33	46	37	38	58	22	52	35	46	49
Total	100	100	100	100	100	100	100	100	100	100	100	100	100	100	100	100

--- Nondurable Goods ---

Quintile of Nondurable Consumption	Total	Food	Alchohol	Housing	Apparel	Transport	Health	Entertainment	Personal Care	Reading	Education	Tobacco	Misc - all qtr	Misc - 5th qtr	Contrib.	Pensions and Life Insurance
Lowest	7	10	7	8	5	6	10	5	8	8	4	13	4	4	5	2
2nd	13	15	14	13	11	12	15	10	13	14	6	19	10	12	10	7
3rd	18	19	17	17	17	19	20	16	19	19	11	22	14	24	14	16
4th	23	22	22	22	24	24	22	23	23	24	19	25	21	25	24	26
Highest	40	34	40	40	43	40	33	47	37	35	61	22	52	35	46	49
Total	100	100	100	100	100	100	100	100	100	100	100	100	100	100	100	100

--- Durable Goods ---

Quintile of Nondurable Consumption	Total	Housing	Apparel	Transport	Health	Entertainment	Reading	Education
Lowest	5	7	2	5	8	4	4	13
2nd	11	12	8	11	14	12	10	13
3rd	22	19	13	24	18	16	15	14
4th	25	23	19	25	23	24	25	21
Highest	37	39	57	35	37	44	46	39
Total	100	100	100	100	100	100	100	100

Table 5c: 1987 Panel Imputation -- Percent Distribution Across Expenditure Quintile

(1987 Expenditure Levels)

--- All Goods ---

Nondurable Consumpt	Total	Food	Alchohol	Housing	Apparel	Transport	Health	Entertainment	Personal Care	Reading	Education	Tobacco	Misc - all qtr	Misc- 5th qtr	Contrib.	Pensions and Life Insurance
Lowest	7	10	10	8	6	6	6	5	7	7	9	15	2	5	7	2
2nd	12	13	17	13	10	13	12	10	13	12	11	19	8	13	7	8
3rd	17	18	16	17	15	19	18	16	18	17	16	20	16	20	14	14
4th	24	23	21	23	23	25	25	24	25	25	14	25	24	26	22	25
Highest	40	36	36	39	46	38	39	45	38	39	50	20	49	36	49	51
Total	100	100	100	100	100	100	100	100	100	100	100	100	100	100	100	100

--- Nondurable Goods ---

Nondurable Consumpt	Total	Food	Alchohol	Housing	Apparel	Transport	Health	Entertainment	Personal Care	Reading	Education	Tobacco	Misc - all qtr	Misc- 5th qtr	Contrib.	Pensions and Life Insurance
Lowest	7	10	10	8	6	6	6	5	7	7	7	15	2	5	7	2
2nd	12	13	17	13	10	12	12	10	13	13	10	19	8	13	7	8
3rd	17	18	16	17	16	18	18	15	18	18	16	20	16	20	14	14
4th	23	23	21	23	23	24	25	24	25	26	14	25	24	26	22	25
Highest	41	36	36	39	45	40	39	46	38	37	53	20	49	36	49	51
Total	100	100	100	100	100	100	100	100	100	100	100	100	100	100	100	100

--- Durable Goods ---

Nondurable Consumpt	Total	Housing	Apparel	Transport	Health	Entertainment	Reading	Education
Lowest	7	8	3	6	7	5	7	22
2nd	12	11	5	14	10	11	10	18
3rd	18	15	13	19	17	17	15	16
4th	25	23	21	25	26	24	25	14
Highest	38	43	58	35	40	44	43	29
Total	100	100	100	100	100	100	100	100

C.1 - 13

Table 5d: 1996 Panel Imputation -- Percent Distribution Across Expenditure Quintile

(1987 Expenditure Levels)

--- All Goods ---

Nondurable Consumpt	Total	Food	Alchohol	Housing	Apparel	Transport	Health	Entertainment	Personal Care	Reading	Education	Tobacco	Misc - all qtr	Misc- 5th qtr	Contrib.	Pensions and Life Insurance
Lowest	7	9	8	8	5	5	8	5	7	7	6	15	3	4	5	3
2nd	12	14	15	13	10	14	11	10	13	12	12	19	8	14	9	8
3rd	17	18	17	18	16	18	17	16	18	17	15	21	16	19	15	14
4th	24	24	22	23	24	25	26	24	25	26	18	23	25	26	24	25
Highest	40	35	38	39	46	38	38	45	37	38	49	22	48	36	48	50
Total	100	100	100	100	100	100	100	100	100	100	100	100	100	100	100	100

--- Nondurable Goods ---

Nondurable Consumpt	Total	Food	Alchohol	Housing	Apparel	Transport	Health	Entertainment	Personal Care	Reading	Education	Tobacco	Misc - all qtr	Misc- 5th qtr	Contrib.	Pensions and Life Insurance
Lowest	7	9	8	8	5	5	8	5	7	7	5	15	3	4	5	3
2nd	12	14	15	13	10	12	11	10	13	12	10	19	8	14	9	8
3rd	17	18	17	18	16	18	17	16	18	18	15	21	16	19	15	14
4th	24	24	22	23	24	25	26	24	25	26	18	23	25	26	24	25
Highest	40	35	38	38	44	40	38	45	37	36	51	22	48	36	48	50
Total	100	100	100	100	100	100	100	100	100	100	100	100	100	100	100	100

--- Durable Goods ---

Nondurable Consumpt	Total	Food	Alchohol	Housing	Apparel	Transport	Health	Entertainment	Personal Care	Reading	Education	Tobacco	Misc - all qtr	Misc- 5th qtr	Contrib.	Pensions and Life Insurance
Lowest	5			8	2	5	8	4		6	15					
2nd	13			10	6	15	12	10		10	20					
3rd	18			16	11	19	17	15		15	16					
4th	25			24	21	25	26	25		25	18					
Highest	39			42	60	36	38	45		43	31					
Total	100			100	100	100	100	100		100	100					

C.1 - 14

Table 6a: Four Quarters of Expenses for CU's Present in 1994(1)-- Percent Distribution Across Expenditure Category

(1987 Expenditure Levels)

Quintile of Nondurable Consumption	Total	Food	Alchohol	Housing	Apparel	Transport	Health	Entertainment	Personal Care	Reading	Education	Tobacco	Misc - all qtr	Misc- 5th qtr	Contrib.	Pensions and Life Insurance
--- All Goods ---																
Lowest	100	24	1	35	4	17	6	4	1	1	1	1	1	1	2	3
2nd	100	20	1	32	4	22	5	4	1	0	1	2	1	1	2	5
3rd	100	17	1	30	4	24	5	4	1	1	1	1	1	1	3	6
4th	100	17	1	30	5	22	4	5	1	1	1	1	1	1	3	8
Highest	100	15	1	31	5	20	4	5	1	0	2	1	1	1	4	10
Total	100	17	1	31	5	21	4	5	1	0	1	1	1	1	3	8
--- Nondurable Goods ---																
Lowest	100	28	1	38	4	9	7	3	1	1	1	2	1	1	2	3
2nd	100	25	1	35	5	11	6	3	1	0	1	2	1	1	3	6
3rd	100	22	1	34	5	12	5	3	1	0	1	2	1	1	4	8
4th	100	21	1	33	5	12	5	4	1	0	1	1	1	1	3	10
Highest	100	18	1	33	6	12	4	4	1	0	2	1	2	1	5	12
Total	100	21	1	34	5	12	5	4	1	0	1	1	1	1	4	10
--- Durable Goods ---																
Lowest	100			21	1	64	2	9		1	2					
2nd	100			18	2	70	1	7		1	1					
3rd	100			14	2	72	1	9		1	0					
4th	100			18	2	67	1	10		1	1					
Highest	100			20	4	62	1	12		1	1					
Total	100			18	3	66	1	10		1	1					

Table 6b: Four Quarters of Expenses for CU's Present in 1995(1)-- Percent Distribution Across Expenditure Category

(1987 Expenditure Levels)

Quintile of Nondurable Consumption	Total	Food	Alchohol	Housing	Apparel	Transport	Health	Entertainment	Personal Care	Reading	Education	Tobacco	Misc - all qtr	Misc- 5th qtr	Contrib.	Pensions and Life Insurance
--- All Goods ---																
Lowest	100	24	1	36	4	16	6	3	1	1	1	2	1	1	2	3
2nd	100	20	1	33	4	19	5	4	1	0	1	2	1	1	3	5
3rd	100	18	1	30	4	24	4	4	1	0	1	1	1	1	2	7
4th	100	17	1	30	5	22	4	5	1	0	1	1	1	1	3	9
Highest	100	15	1	32	5	19	3	5	1	0	1	1	2	1	4	10
Total	100	17	1	31	5	21	4	5	1	0	1	1	1	1	3	8
--- Nondurable Goods ---																
Lowest	100	28	1	37	4	9	6	2	1	0	1	2	1	1	3	3
2nd	100	24	1	36	4	11	6	3	1	0	1	2	1	1	3	6
3rd	100	22	1	33	5	12	5	3	1	0	1	1	1	2	3	9
4th	100	20	1	33	5	12	4	3	1	0	1	1	1	1	4	11
Highest	100	18	1	34	6	11	4	4	1	0	2	1	2	1	4	12
Total	100	21	1	34	5	11	5	3	1	0	1	1	1	1	4	10
--- Durable Goods ---																
Lowest	100			26	1	61	2	8	0	1	2					
2nd	100			20	2	65	2	10	0	1	1					
3rd	100			16	1	73	1	7	0	1	0					
4th	100			17	2	69	1	10	0	1	1					
Highest	100			19	4	63	1	11	0	1	1					
Total	100			18	2	67	1	10	0	1	1					

Table 6c: 1987 Panel Imputation -- Percent Distribution Across Expenditure Category

(1987 Expenditure Levels)

Quintile of Nondurable Consumption	Total	Food	Alchohol	Housing	Apparel	Transport	Health	Entertainment	Personal Care	Reading	Education	Tobacco	Misc - all qtr	Misc- 5th qtr	Contrib.	Pensions and Life Insurance
--- All Goods ---																
Lowest	100	23	2	35	4	18	4	4	1	0	2	1	0	1	3	3
2nd	100	19	2	34	4	22	4	4	1	0	1	1	1	1	2	5
3rd	100	17	1	32	4	23	4	4	1	0	1	1	1	1	3	6
4th	100	17	1	31	5	21	4	5	1	1	1	1	1	1	3	8
Highest	100	15	1	31	6	19	4	5	1	0	2	0	1	1	4	10
Total	100	17	1	32	5	20	4	5	1	0	1	1	1	1	3	8
--- Nondurable Goods ---																
Lowest	100	27	2	38	4	9	4	3	1	0	1	2	0	1	4	3
2nd	100	23	2	37	5	12	4	3	1	0	1	1	1	1	2	6
3rd	100	21	1	35	5	12	5	3	1	0	1	1	1	1	3	8
4th	100	20	1	34	5	12	5	4	1	0	1	1	1	1	4	10
Highest	100	17	1	33	6	11	4	4	1	0	2	0	2	1	5	12
Total	100	20	1	34	5	11	4	4	1	0	1	1	1	1	4	10
--- Durable Goods ---																
Lowest	100			22	1	64	2	8		1	3					
2nd	100			16	1	71	1	9		1	1					
3rd	100			16	2	70	1	10		1	1					
4th	100			17	2	67	2	10		1	1					
Highest	100			21	4	60	1	12		1	1					
Total	100			18	3	65	1	10		1	1					

C.1 - 17

Table 6d: 1996 Panel Imputation -- Percent Distribution Across Expenditure Category

(1987 Expenditure Levels)

Quintile of Nondurable Consumption	Total	Food	Alchohol	Housing	Apparel	Transport	Health	Entertain ment	Personal Care	Reading	Education	Tobacco	Misc - all qtr	Misc- 5th qtr	Contrib.	Pensions and Life Insurance
								--- All Goods ---								
Lowest	100	24	1	37	4	16	4	3	1	1	1	2	1	1	2	3
2nd	100	19	1	34	4	22	3	4	1	0	1	1	1	1	2	5
3rd	100	18	1	33	4	22	4	4	1	0	1	1	1	1	3	7
4th	100	16	1	31	5	21	4	5	1	1	1	1	1	1	3	8
Highest	100	15	1	31	6	19	4	5	1	0	1	0	1	1	4	10
Total	100	17	1	32	5	20	4	5	1	0	1	1	1	1	3	8
								--- Nondurable Goods ---								
Lowest	100	28	1	39	4	9	5	3	1	0	1	2	1	1	2	4
2nd	100	23	2	38	5	12	4	3	1	0	1	1	1	1	3	6
3rd	100	21	1	36	5	12	4	3	1	0	1	1	1	1	3	8
4th	100	20	1	34	5	12	5	4	1	0	1	1	1	1	4	10
Highest	100	18	1	33	6	11	4	4	1	0	1	0	2	1	4	12
Total	100	20	1	35	5	11	4	4	1	0	1	1	1	1	4	10
								--- Durable Goods ---								
Lowest	100			26	1	59	2	8		1	2					
2nd	100			15	1	73	1	8		1	1					
3rd	100			17	2	69	1	9		1	1					
4th	100			18	2	67	1	10		1	1					
Highest	100			20	4	61	1	12		1	1					
Total	100			19	3	65	1	10		1	1					

Table 7a: 4 Quarters of Expenses for 1994(1)- -- Distribution of Goods Subject to Excise Across Expenditure Quintiles

(1987 Expenditure Levels)

Quintile of Nondurable Consumption	Goods Subject to Excise	Alcohol	Airline	Gasoline	Telephone	Tobacco
--- Percent Across Quintile ---						
Lowest	8	7	2	7	11	10
2nd	14	12	8	14	16	19
3rd	19	17	11	19	20	22
4th	25	24	22	26	23	26
Highest	35	41	57	34	30	23
Total	100	100	100	100	100	100
--- Percent of Total Nondurable Expenditures ---						
Lowest	11	1	0	4	3	2
2nd	12	1	1	5	3	2
3rd	11	1	1	5	3	2
4th	10	1	1	4	2	1
Highest	8	1	2	3	2	1
Total	10	1	1	4	2	1

Table 7b: 4 Quarters of Expenses for 1995(1)- -- Distribution of Goods Subject to Excise Across Expenditure Quintiles

(1987 Expenditure Levels)

Quintile of Nondurable Consumption	Goods Subject to Excise	Alcohol	Airline	Gasoline	Telephone	Tobacco
--- Percent Across Quintile ---						
Lowest	8	7	2	8	10	13
2nd	15	14	6	15	17	19
3rd	20	17	14	21	20	22
4th	23	22	21	24	23	25
Highest	34	40	57	32	29	22
Total	100	100	100	100	100	100
--- Percent of Total Nondurable Expenditures ---						
Lowest	11	1	0	4	3	2
2nd	12	1	1	5	3	2
3rd	11	1	1	5	2	1
4th	10	1	1	4	2	1
Highest	8	1	2	3	2	1
Total	10	1	1	4	2	1

Table 7c: 1987 Panel Imputation -- Distribution of Goods Subject to Excise Across Expenditure Quintiles

(1987 Expenditure Levels)

Quintile of Nondurable Consumption	Goods Subject to Excise	Alcohol	Airline	Gasoline	Telephone	Tobacco
--- Percent Across Quintile ---						
Lowest	9	10	2	8	10	15
2nd	14	17	7	14	16	19
3rd	19	16	14	20	20	20
4th	23	21	22	25	23	25
Highest	35	36	55	33	30	20
Total	100	100	100	100	100	100
--- Percent of Total Nondurable Expenditures ---						
Lowest	11	2	0	4	3	2
2nd	11	2	1	4	3	1
3rd	10	1	1	4	3	1
4th	9	1	1	4	2	1
Highest	8	1	2	3	2	0
Total	9	1	1	4	2	1

Table 7d: 1996 Panel Imputation -- Distribution of Goods Subject to Excise Across Expenditure Quintiles

(1987 Expenditure Levels)

Quintile of Nondurable Consumption	Goods Subject to Excise	Alcohol	Airline	Gasoline	Telephone	Tobacco
--- Level ($ millions) ---						
Lowest	21,003	2,808	714	7,889	6,132	3,460
2nd	37,461	5,450	2,420	15,173	10,238	4,180
3rd	47,955	6,019	4,584	20,177	12,366	4,809
4th	61,061	7,672	7,840	26,157	14,123	5,269
Highest	89,428	13,543	18,427	34,618	17,977	4,863
Total	256,908	35,491	33,986	104,014	60,835	22,582
--- Percent Across Quintile ---						
Lowest	8	8	2	8	10	15
2nd	15	15	7	15	17	19
3rd	19	17	13	19	20	21
4th	24	22	23	25	23	23
Highest	35	38	54	33	30	22
Total	100	100	100	100	100	100

APPENDIX C.2

Imputations: Tuition Expenses for Postsecondary Education

by

James Cilke

and

Julie-Anne Cronin

Tuition Expenses for Postsecondary Education

I. The Data

We used two micro-data sources to impute tuition expenses for postsecondary education. These imputations were needed to properly simulate the two tax credits for higher education expenses as well as the temporary above-the-line deduction for education expenses. The first file, produced by the Department of Education, was the 1995-1996 National Postsecondary Student Aid Study (NPSAS). This file contained the results of a survey of postsecondary students which asked a multitude of questions about the financial and demographic characteristics of students and their parents, the types of degrees or certificates they were seeking, and the attributes of the schools they were attending. The second file was an extract from the 1999 INSOLE file and contained tax information for people who either received a 1098T Information Return or who filled out Form 8863 to claim a credit for higher education expenses.

A. The NPSAS

The first step in the imputation process was to extract certain specific pieces of information from the NPSAS. The NPSAS is very rich in information about higher education but did not include everything we needed to impute student status to panel members. Further, like most survey studies, some important data items were missing for some records. In general, missing values were assumed to be random events and therefore imputed in the same proportions as non-missing values.

A number of variables were estimated using the NPSAS data. The AGI of independent students and the AGI of parents of dependent students were estimated as total (cash) income less Social Security transfers,[1] AFDC payments, other non-taxable transfers and child support payments. Whether or not a married student was the primary taxpayer was estimated based on whether or not the student had more earnings than his/her spouse. The higher earner was assigned primary status. In cases where the earnings were the same or zero, the male was assigned primary status.

Four variables were created to indicate a person's status as a student. The first variable (ISTART) indicated whether a student was in their first year of higher education. A second variable (ILASTYR) indicated whether a student was in their last year of higher education. A third variable (BGRAD) indicated whether a graduating high school senior would become a beginning graduate student in the following year. Finally, a fourth variable (ITOGO) indicated the number of additional years the student would attend a higher education institution

---

[1] The level of Social Security benefits in AGI could also have been estimated but its omission is unlikely to have affected our results. Ultimately, we wanted to create a variable for AGI class. Taxable Social Security benefits were unlikely to move a high income return to another income class and benefits are not taxable at the low end.

ISTART was set to 1 if the student was a first year freshman, a first year graduate student, enrolled in less than a two year program, or in the process of changing from an undergraduate to a graduate student. (Starting graduate students were treated as starting students, even if they were in school in the previous year.) ILASTYR was set to 1 if the student was a graduating senior or was receiving his degree, or if the student's own plans for the following year did not include going to school. BGRAD was set to 1 for graduating seniors and other degree earners who also indicated that they were planning on attending school in the following year.

Everybody who was not in their last year was given at least one additional year of higher education to go. Undergraduates in a traditional 2-year program or less were initially assumed to have one remaining year to go. Undergraduates in traditional 4-year programs were initially assumed to have either one, two, or three additional years of education to go, depending on whether the student classified himself as a junior, sophomore, or freshman. Starting graduate students in a Masters program were assigned two additional years, while continuing Masters students were assigned one additional year. Beginning graduate students in either a Ph.D. program or other professional program were initially assigned four additional years to go (ITOGO=4). Otherwise ITOGO for Ph.D. and other students in professional programs was set to 5 minus the number of years completed, but not less than one. For all other graduate students, ITOGO was set to 2 for beginning students and 1 for continuing students.

The last group of students who needed an imputation for the amount of time remaining were graduating high school seniors who were immediately continuing on to a postsecondary school. We calculated the distribution of ITOGO for all starting postsecondary students and applied this distribution to the group of continuing seniors.

After the initial assignment of ITOGO, a few adjustments were made. First, if the person was less than a half-time student, then ITOGO doubled. Next, 30% of all students with 3 or more years to go, 20% of all students with 2 year to go, and 10% of student with 1 year to go were randomly assigned an additional year to go.

B. The 1999 INSOLE File

From the population of tax returns filed for tax year 1999, SOI drew a sample of approximately 177,000 returns. This sample was extensively edited, and weighted to represent the population of tax returns filed for 1999.[2] The SOI sample included both dependent (approximately 7,000) and non-dependent (approximately 170,000) returns. Dependent returns were sampled independently from their parent returns. To prevent double counting, we only worked with non-dependent returns.[3]

---

[2] More technically, the sample represented individual tax returns filed in processing year 2000. For more information on SOI's sampling methodology, see "Individual Income Tax Returns 1999," published by the Internal Revenue Service.

[3] All dependent students were represented on the non-dependent return on which they were claimed.

For each non-dependent tax return, we extracted a set of items found on Form 1040, the primary individual income tax return form, and Form 8863, the form used to compute the tax return's education credit.[4] We supplemented our SOI data with data reported on Form 1098t.

Because 1098ts are issued by all postsecondary institutions (eligible for Title IV funds) to their enrolled students, these forms allowed us to identify the postsecondary student population in the tax data.   In addition, the 1098t's contained a taxpayer identification number (TIN) for the issuing school, and information on the individual's level of enrollment (graduate or undergraduate) and time commitment (less than half-time or at least half-time). By exactly matching the 1098ts to the tax returns, we were able to compare the pool of potentially credit-eligible students (those who received a 1098t) to those for whom an education credit was actually taken (those who appeared on a Form 8863). Using the school identifier, we determined the type (two-year or four-year) and control (public or private) of the school attended. Of the 170,000 non-dependent returns in our sample, approximately 24,000 (14 percent) received at least one 1098t.[5]

II. Statistical Match Between the Tax File and the NPSAS.

The next step in the imputation process was to statistically match the file of higher-education students derived from the 1999 INSOLE file with the NPSAS data. Two unconstrained statistical matches were performed; one for students who were dependents of others and another for independent students.[6] In the case of dependent students, the initial matching variables were:

- Age of student,
- 7 age classes of the student's (primary) parent[7],
- 14 AGI classes of the student's parent,
- Marital status of the student's parent(s),
- Number of dependents exemptions claimed by parents[8],
- Graduate student status,

---

[4] From Form 1040 we obtained most of the income fields, certain deductions used to offset total income, and most of the tax liability and tax credit fields. We also obtained filing status (joint, non-joint), type of form (1040, 1040A, 1040EZ), number of dependents, and the return's population weight. For each return that included a Form 8863, we obtained most of the items on that form. These items included total qualified Hope expenses, total qualified lifetime learning expenses, their combined credit amounts, and the credit remaining after applying phase-out and tax liability limitations. Approximately 5,000 tax returns in the sample included a Form 8863.

[5] A single return may receive more than one 1098t, and an individual on a return can receive multiple 1098ts (for example if he or she transferred during the course of the year or moved from undergraduate to post-graduate education). Among those returns that received at least one 1098t, 83 percent received only one, 15 percent received two, and 2 percent received three or more.   Approximately 24,000 individuals in our sample received at least one 1098t. Among those individuals, 86 percent received only one, 12 percent received two, and 2 percent received three or more.

[6] Dependency here was defined according to tax rules, not the financial aid rules set the Department of Education.

[7] Age classes for the student's parent were Under 45, 45-49, 50-54, 55-59, 60-64, 65-69, and 70 and older.

[8] Dependent classes were 1, 2-4, and 5 or more.

- Type of graduate student program[9],
- Full time versus part time status, and
- Private vs. public schools.

All tax records were matched to a NPSAS record. Each tax record and each NPSAS record was placed into a unique matching cell. For every two identically-defined matching cells, the first tax record was linked with the first NPSAS record; the second tax record was linked to the second NPSAS record, and so on until all of the tax records were matched. If the tax cell had more records than the NPSAS cell, the process was repeated after the last NPSAS record was used.

In some cases, there were no NPSAS records that had the same matching characteristics as a tax record cell. In these cases, the matching cells needed to be expanded. We first expanded cells by eliminating the cells defined by the number of dependent exemptions claimed by the student's parents. Next we eliminated the cells defined by the AGI class of the student's parents. In the next pass, we allowed for students on the tax file to match with NPSAS students with a 1 year age difference. We also eliminated distinctions based on the age of the parent and the marital status of the parent, and the type of graduate school program. With these expansions, nearly all tax records were matched. In the final pass, we used matching cells defined by type of school (public vs. private), attendance intensity (full vs. part time) and level of program (graduate vs. undergraduate).

The matching process for independent students was the same. The variables used to define the matching cells for independent students were:

- 9 age of student classes[10],
- 14 AGI of the student classes,[11]
- Marital status of the student,[12]
- Number of dependents exemptions claimed by the student (zero or 1 or more),
- Graduate student status,
- Type of graduate student program,
- Full time vs. part time status, and
- Private vs. Public schools.

Like the match with dependent students, the cell expansions first occurred by eliminating the distinction for number of dependent exemptions. The AGI class of the student distinction was then eliminated. With this expansion, all but 6 non-dependent tax records were matched.

Once these matches were complete, there were two linked data files, one for students who were dependents of others and one for non-dependent students. The combined number of

---

[9] Graduate student programs were classified into two types; regular and professional. Professional programs largely consisted of medical programs and legal programs.

[10] Classes were, in years, under 20, 20-21, 22-23, 24-29, 30-34, 35-39, 40-49, 50-64, and 65 and over.

[11] Same classes as AGI of Parents.

[12] The categories were joint primary, joint secondary, and non-joint.

records was exactly equal to the number of records on the tax extract file of students taken from the 1999 INSOLE file. These NPSAS-Tax files were used to impute student status and tuition expenses to panel members.

III. Statistical Match between 2004 panel records and the NPSAS-Tax File

The next step in this process was to statistically match people on the panel to students on the matched NPSAS-Tax file. The first step was to build extracts of potential students from 2004 panel records. Three types of potential students were extracted: dependents of other taxpayers, independent spouses on joint returns, and independent primaries on panel returns[13]. All non-dependent people on the panel in 2004 and all dependents age 16 or over were eligible to receive an education imputation.

The following variables were used in the statistical match between dependent students.

- Age of Student,
- 7 Age classes of the student's (primary) parent,
- 14 AGI classes of the student's parent[14],
- Wages as a percent of AGI on parent's return.[15]

The following variables were used in the statistical match between spouses on joint returns.

- Age of Student[16],
- 14 AGI classes,
- Wages as a percent of AGI classes,
- Wages earned by student,[17]
- With dependent children flag.

The following variables were used in the statistical match between non-dependent primaries[18].

- Age of Student,
- 14 AGI classes,
- Wages as a percent of AGI classes,
- Wages earned by student,
- With dependent children flag,

---

[13] It was not necessary to split independent primaries between joint returns and non-joint returns because marital status was used as a hard matching variable.

[14] Age classes and AGI classes for the student's parents in this match were the same as used in the earlier match. See footnotes 2 and 3.

[15] Wages as a percent of AGI classes were: >100%, 95%-100%, 90%-95%, 75%-90%, 50%-75%, 25%-50%, 0%-25%, and exactly 0%.

[16] For students aged 50 or more, the student's age was rounded to an even number.

[17] Wages of the student classes were (in thousands): zero, 0-5, 5-10, 10-20, and over 20.

[18] Same definitions as used in the match to non-dependent spouses.

– Filing status (joint vs. non-joint).

Based on tabulations from the 1999 tax file of students, the number of dependent students attending a higher-education institution in 1999 was approximately 6.7 million. The number of spouses on joint returns was approximately 3.3 million and the number of non-dependent primaries was 9.4 million. These three values became the targets for the statistical match.

Similar to the previous matches, each panel record and each NPSAS-Tax record were placed into a unique matching cell. For every two identically-defined matching cells, one holding panel records and the other holding NPSAS-Tax records, the first panel record was linked with the first NPSAS-Tax record. However, this time, the weight of the panel record was subtracted from the weight of the NPSAS-Tax record. If the weight of the NPSAS-Tax record was still positive, it was available for a second match. The same NPSAS-Tax record was then matched to the next panel record in the cell. Conversely, if the weight on the NPSAS-Tax record was reduced to zero, then the next NPSAS-Tax record was used in the cell. This process insured that nearly all of the NPSAS-Tax records within a cell were used in the match.

When matching to spouses and to non-dependent primaries, only a single pass through each file was needed. The matching cells did not need to be expanded. Further, the number of students on the matched file was very close to the target number of students.

When matching to dependents, the matching cells needed to be expanded. First, the age of the student's parent for students aged 25 and higher was dropped. Next the number of classes for the age of the student's parents was reduced to 4 and the number of AGI classes were cut in half and the number of wages as a percent of AGI classes were cut in half.

Student Information Carried to the Panel. With the match of 2004 panel persons completed, the next step was to carry the matched student information to the panel. The variables carried and linked from the NPSAS-Tax file to the matched panel records included (but were not limited to):

– A pointer to the NPSAS file,
– A pointer to the 1999 INSOLE student tax file,
– A graduate/undergraduate student indicator,
– An indicator for the length of the undergraduate program (2 or 4-year, other)
– An indicator for the current level of the undergraduate student (freshman, sophomore, junior, senior, or other),
– An indicator for the kind of undergraduate "degree" being sought (certificate, associates degree, bachelors degree, or non-degree).
– An indicator for the kind of graduate program for the student (regular, professional, or other)
– An indicator for the kind of graduate "degree" being sought (masters, Ph.D., "professional", and other)

- A public/private school indicator,
- A full-time/part-time attendance indicator,
- An in-state/out-of-state student indicator,
- A flag indicating whether the actual student in 1999 was apparently eligible for an education credit but failed to take the credit.
- A flag indicating the student receives a Pell Grant.
- The number of years of study remaining,
- An indicator for just-starting students,
- An indicator for students in their final year,

IV. Imputing Student Status to 2005 to 2013 records

At this point, we had a student indicator imputation for people on the panel in 2004. Using the years-of-study remaining variable, we had also imputed their student-status in the following year and beyond.[19] For many students, 2004 was their final year of study. So, we needed a student indicator for people beginning school after 2004.

To accomplish this, we largely repeated the statistical matching process used to impute student status for 2004. First, we determined how many beginning students were needed to hit our targets in a particular year. We then extracted potential students from the panel. The only additional criteria was that the person could not have been a student in the current year or the prior year.[20] An almost identical matching methodology was used to link new beginning students to the NPSAS-TAX file. One difference was that only starting students from the NPSAS-Tax file were matched. Another difference is that a match usually produced too many students. So, among the pool of successful matches, just enough students in each of the three categories were randomly selected to hit the target number of students for the match. The student population was expected to grow during the 2004-2013 period by, on average, by 1.4% per year.

V. Imputing Tuition Values

Tuition values were imputed to the panel model according to the level and control of the student's institution and whether or not the student lived in or out of state. In-state tuition amounts at public and private institutions also varied by state, as given in the *Digest of Education Statistics* (see attached Table). For 4-year out-of-state private tuition, we used 3 values; 30% of such students paid $11,500 (in 1999 dollars), 40% paid $14,500, and 30% paid $19,500. We assumed that all out-of-state students at 4-year public institutions paid the median 4-year public tuition of $9000 or the average 2 year public tuition of $7182 per year, respectively. Tuition values for 25% of students attending school half-time or more were reduced by 50% to roughly approximate students attending more than half time but less than full-time. Tuition values for less than half-time students were

---

[19] The imputation process assumed the student would remain in school for as long as the years-remaining variable suggested, regardless of the possible changing circumstances of the student (except death).

[20] Its entirely possible a person who was a student two years prior to the current year to be imputed a student status a second time. Further, we did not control the kind or type of student the person could be on his second imputation.

reduced by 75 percent. Values for students in their first or last year of study were reduced by 50%. The imputed values of tuition were forecasted to grow over time by tuition specific inflation indices that varied by the institution's level and control (e.g. tuition at 2 year public institutions was generally forecasted to grow at a slower rate than tuition at 4-year public institutions). The forecasted values were based on historical data from the College Board and ITM projections.

Average Tuition 1999-2000 Academic Year for Full Time Equivalent Students by Level, Control and State*

| | 4 year | | | | 2 year | | | | |
| | Public | | Private | | Public | | | | 1st |
	In State	Out of State	In State	Out of State	In State	Out of State	Private	Grad	Professional
National average	3,290	8,640	14,301		1,330	4,521	7,182	13,500	22,000
Low (bottom 30 %)				11,500					
Medium (middle 40%)				14,500					
High (top 30%)				19,500					
Median		9,000							
By State:									
Alabama	2,727	8,403	8,697		1,504	4,571	8,383		
Alaska	2,808	9,627	8,320		1,998	5,777	7,182		
Arizona	2,205	9,024	7,539		879	4,658	7,182		
Arkansas	2,684	7,564	8,157		1,020	2,698	5,448		
California	2,588	9,407	14,784		357	4,136	7,182		
Colorado	2,731	9,550	13,124		1,561		7,182		
Connecticuit	4,394	10,392	19,352		1,853	6,077	14,332		
Delaware	4,562	9,009	8,007		1,528	4,479	9,139		
DistCol	2,040	6,487	17,606		1,330	4,397	8,383		
Florida	2,134	7,810	12,282		1,319	4,386	8,383		
Georgia	2,489	8,165	12,275		1,295	4,362	8,383		
Hawaii	2,919	9,738	7,320		1,028	4,807	7,182		
Idaho	2,420	9,239	12,490		1,220	4,999	7,182		
Illinois	3,941	8,998	14,364		1,463	4,863	7,583		
Indiana	3,570	8,627	15,077		2,126	5,526	7,583		
Iowa	2,934	7,991	13,708		2,021	5,421			
Kansas	2,416	7,473	10,405		1,327	4,727	7,583		
Kentucky	2,620	8,296	9,394		1,279	4,346	8,383		
Louisiana	2,410	8,086	14,293		901	3,968	8,383		
Maine	4,094	10,092	20,218		2,712	6,936	14,332		
Maryland	4,455	8,902	17,432		2,256	5,207	9,139		
Massachusetts	4,064	10,062	19,611		2,024	6,248	14,332		
Michigan	4,403	9,460	10,399		1,714	5,114	7,583		
Minnesota	3,818	8,875	15,252		2,367	5,767	7,583		
Mississippi	2,866	8,542	8,585		968	4,035	8,383		
Missouri	3,628	8,685	11,481		1,427	4,827	7,583		
Montana	2,904	9,723	8,765		1,926	5,705	7,182		
Nebraska	2,779	7,836	10,990		1,361	4,761	7,583		
Nevada	1,997	8,816	7,372		1,189	4,968	7,182		
New Hampshire	5,917	11,915	16,142		3,725	7,949	14,332		
New Jersey	5,105	9,552	15,982		2,102	5,053	9,139		
New Mexico	2,262	7,142	9,787		736	2,414	5,448		
New York	3,948	8,395	19,927		2,549	5,500	9,139		
North Carolina	2,007	7,683	15,756		682	3,749	8,383		
North Dakota	2,840	7,897	9,156		1,867	5,267	7,583		
Ohio	4,375	9,432	14,471		2,417	5,817	7,583		
Oklahoma	2,128	7,008	9,642		1,216	2,894	5,448		
Oregon	3,571	10,390	16,124		1,607	5,386	7,182		
Pennsylvania	5,473	9,920	16,682		2,140	5,091	9,139		
Rhode Island	4,242	10,240	17,275		1,746	5,970	14,332		
South Carolina	3,577	9,253	11,636		1,279	4,346	8,383		
South Dakota	3,124	8,181	10,508		2,687	6,087	7,583		
Tennessee	2,598	8,274	11,841		1,276	4,343	8,383		
Texas	2,538	7,418	13,288		893	2,571	5,448		
Utah	2,150	8,969	3,463		1,480	5,259	7,182		
Vermont	6,845	12,843	17,989		2,781	7,005	14,332		
Virginia	3,948	9,624	12,464		1,273	4,340	8,383		
Washington	3,253	10,072	14,670		1,620	5,399	7,182		
West Virginia	2,444	7,501	11,954		1,526	4,926	7,583		
Wisconsin	3,213	8,270	13,900		2,117	5,517	7,583		
Wyoming	2,373	9,192	14,301		1,278	5,057	7,182		

Source: *Digest of Education Statistics*

* Data in bold was used in the model.

APPENDIX C.3

Imputations: Health Insurance Status

by

Gillian Hunter

and

Emily Lin

Health Insurance Status

I. Summary

Health insurance coverage and premium amounts were imputed to the model to enable the model to analyze the effect of a wide variety of tax and health reform proposals. Employer-provided health coverage and tax-preferred premium amounts were needed to analyze the effect of current law tax preferences. In addition, nongroup insurance coverage and premiums, out-of-pocket expenses, public coverage and uninsured status were needed to analyze the effects of reform proposals including newly proposed tax deductions, exclusions and credits.

Because no single health survey includes the necessary items, a variety of surveys were linked together through matching techniques. First, data from the 1997 Robert Wood Johnson Foundation Employer Health Insurance Survey[1] (RWJF) were statistically matched using employer and employee characteristics to the Current Population Survey (CPS) to determine premiums, employer and employee contributions, and other plan characteristics for employer-provided health insurance. Then data from the CPS (with the matched RWJF variables) were matched to the panel in order to determine who is covered by employer, nongroup, Medicare and Medicaid health insurance and to identify the residual category of uninsured individuals. Nongroup health insurance premiums from the National Health Insurance Survey (NHIS) were assigned to individuals in the nongroup market. Finally, data from the Medical Expenditure Panel Survey (MEPS) were used to impute out-of-pocket medical expenditures. Tax data already on the panel provided information on itemized medical expenses and the above-the-line deduction for health insurance for self-employed individuals.

II. Matching the RWJF Employer-Provided Health Insurance Variables to the CPS

Data from the RWJF, including employer-provided health insurance premiums, employees' share of the premium and other plan characteristics (e.g., out-of-pocket limit), were statistically matched to the individuals identified as policyholders of employer plans in the CPS. The RWJF variables were then brought over to the Panel Model through the statistical match from the CPS to the Panel Model.

A. The RWJF Survey

The RWJF is a national probability sample of public employers and private establishments. For public employers, the data indicate whether the government is a federal, state, or local agency. For private establishments, the RWJF contains information about the industry of the employer and the size of the firm. The survey also collects information on the distribution of the hourly wage paid to the employees and

---

[1] Premiums from the employer survey in the MEPS were not used, because there was no way to link premiums to family income. The RWJF survey included both premiums and wage data, enabling a link since wages are the major component of income.

whether the employer offers health insurance. If health insurance is offered by an employer, the data have information about the number of plans offered and, for each plan, the monthly premium for the single and family policy, the employees' share of the premium, the number of workers enrolled in the plan, and the share of the enrollees in the single and family policy.

B. Matching Cells - RWJF

The following four variables from the RWJF and CPS were used to define the matching cells:

1.   Policy type: single or family;

2.   Industry and employment sector: 9 private industries and 3 levels of governments;

3.   Firm size (applicable only for private-sector employers): fewer than 10 workers, 10-24 workers, 25-99 workers , 100-499 workers, 500-999 workers, or more than 1,000 workers; and

4.   Hourly wage: below $7, $7-$10, $10-$15, and $15 or over (in 1997 dollars).

The CPS sample selected for the match consisted of private- and public-sector employees who participated in their employer's health insurance plan.

The data were adjusted in several ways to facilitate the match. First, because the nine major industries in the RWJF were grouped by the establishments' two-digit SIC codes and the CPS used the 2002 NAICS codes, certain re-mappings between the two industry coding systems were created.

Second, firm size was top coded at 25,000 in the RWJF, and, for these establishments, the industry variable was missing. To deal with the missing-industry problem, the fraction of RWJF policyholders in the largest-firm category who had an unknown industry was calculated (separately for single and family policies), then the same percentage of CPS policyholders in the largest-firm category was randomly selected and a separate statistical match was conducted for these policyholders. Because all of these workers were employed in large private establishments, the matching cells in this case were defined by the type of policy and hourly wage.

Third, the RWJF included a wage category of below $5, but a small percentage of policyholders were classified in this category. To reduce the number of thin cells, the two wage categories, below $5 and $5-$7, were combined.

Fourth, wages in the RWJF file were in 1997 dollars whereas the CPS wages were in 2004 dollars. Instead of indexing the RWJF wage cutoffs to the 2004 level, we calculated, within each RWJF policy-type-industry-firm-size cell (i.e., non-wage partitions), the percentage of policyholders in each of the four wage categories, below $7,

$7-\$10, \$10-\$15, and \$15 and over. Based on this wage distribution, the CPS policyholders in the corresponding cell were ranked by their wages and assigned into the four wage categories.

Cells with small unweighted CPS counts (fewer than 20 in general) were combined with similar cells for better matching results. Small cells were combined with the next cell along the wage and/or firm size dimension to increase the cell size, and cells were never combined across industries, employment sectors, or types of policy.

C. Matching the Records - RWJF

The RWJF data were re-arranged so that each record represented a policy (single or family) of a health plan in a wage category. The RWJF and CPS records were grouped into the matching cells as defined above and randomly ordered within a cell. Each RWJF record carried the plan data and a policyholder count calculated as the number of employees enrolled in the policy who were in the specific wage category. Based on this policyholder count, each RWJF record was given a ranked percentile within the cell. To match the RWJF records to the CPS file, a CPS record received a random draw from a uniform distribution and was matched to the RWJ record with the nearest ranked percentile in the matching cell. An unconstrained match was conducted: The matched file had all the CPS records, but the RWJ records were not required to be used up and could be repeatedly used.

III. Matching CPS Health Coverage Variables to the Family Panel

Then data from the CPS (with the matched RWJ plan variables) were statistically matched to the panel in order to impute health insurance coverage.

A. The CPS Survey

The CPS is a national probability sample of about 60,000 households. The March 2004 CPS ASEC (Annual Social and Economic Supplement) survey asks respondents to identify each type of health insurance coverage (employer, nongroup, Medicare, Medicaid, SCHIP, and several other types of public coverage) for each household member during the preceding calendar year.[2] Individuals who are not reported as having coverage are assigned to the residual category of uninsured.

B. Matching Cells - CPS

Both Panel Model records and CPS records were divided into cells by family type, gender, age, and employment status.

Family Types. Family types included singles, head of household with children, joint filers without children and joint filers with children. Single and head of household filers

---

[2] Some have questioned whether respondents report coverage for the previous year or whether they may erroneously report current coverage.

were sub-divided by gender. Nonfilers and CPS records were put into similar categories. This required changing from the CPS family unit to a tax unit. Subfamilies and adult family members who were not a head of household or a spouse were put into their own separate units. For the Panel Model, independent filers who can be claimed as child dependents were included only as child dependents. Adult dependents were excluded from the analysis.

Age Types. The age categories were: <25, 25-34, 35-44, 45-54, 55-64, 65+.[3] Single and head of household filers were put into the appropriate age category. Joint filers were divided into four categories: both filers under age 65; both filers 65 or older; male head under 65 but female head 65 or older; and male head 65 or older but female head under 65. If both filers were under age 65, the unit was grouped in the appropriate age category by the age of the older filer.

Employment Status. Because the majority of individuals under 65 who have health insurance are covered by employer plans, employment is an important factor in health insurance coverage. In addition, the tax treatment of employer-provided health insurance differs from the tax treatment of health insurance purchased by self-employed individuals.[4] As a result, self-employed individuals needed to be matched separately from other employed individuals. Hence, tax-filing-units were divided sequentially into one of four employment categories: self-employed claiming a health insurance deduction, self-employed but not claiming a health insurance deduction, employed or not employed.

In the tax panel, wages were based on the combined annual wages (and pension contributions reported on a W-2) of both filers for joint returns. Self-employment income reported on schedule SE (i.e., net farm income plus net nonfarm income) was determined on a return basis. In the CPS wages were similarly based on the combined annual wages (but did not include pension contributions) of the head of household and his, or her, spouse. Self-employment income as reported in the CPS was aggregated across the head of household and the spouse but only one of these individuals was required to have positive self-employment income for the unit to be categorized as self-employed.

The tax panel self-employed health insurance deduction amount was used to determine nongroup[5] health insurance coverage and premiums for the self-employed. The CPS was used to assign all other health insurance statuses.

Tax-filing units with positive self-employment income claiming a self-employed health insurance deduction were matched to CPS units with positive self-employed income and nongroup insurance. These units were classified as self-employed with nongroup

---

[3] If both filers were 65 or older or if a singe filer was 65 or older, an additional age break at 85 years was added for tax-filers classified as not employed. See below for discussion of employment status.
[4] Employee contributions to health insurance made through a Section 125 cafeteria plan and employer contributions are excluded from an employee's taxable income for employment and income tax purposes. In contrast, self-employed individuals may under certain circumstances deduct premiums for health insurance regardless of whether they itemize but only up to the amount of their self-employed income.
[5] For ease of exposition, these policies are referred to as nongroup health insurance; however health insurance that is not subsidized by an employer is a more accurate description.

insurance. Otherwise if self-employment income was positive, if wages plus self-employed income exceeded a dollar threshold ($1,000 in $2003), and if self-employed income exceeded a percentage threshold (40 percent of the sum of self-employment income and wages), a unit was classified as self-employed but without nongroup health insurance. If a unit did not fit into these first two categories, then it was classified as a wage earning tax-filing unit if the sum of self-employment income and wages exceeded the dollar threshold. Otherwise a tax-filing unit was classified as "not employed".[6]

Cell Aggregation. In general, cells with fewer than 500 observations were collapsed into larger cells across age, gender, and employment status. A family can have multiple kinds of health insurance (employer-provided, nongroup, Medicare, Medicaid etc.) or multiple policies (both employers may provide health coverage). In addition, a family may insure all, some or none of its family members. As a result, the cells were collapsed in a way that preserved the most common combinations. Because virtually all individuals 65 or older are eligible for Medicare, tax filing units with an aged head (>=65) were not aggregated with those without an aged head. Because the health insurance decision is very different for singles than for married couples and different for couples with children than for couples without children, tax filing units with one head were not aggregated with units with two heads and tax filing units with children were not aggregated with units without children. As expected, nonaged tax filers classified as wage earners had more observations and hence finer age breaks, as did childless tax filers over 65 years of age who were classified as not employed.

C. Matching the Records - CPS

A tax unit's wages as well as total income is likely to affect the decision to purchase health insurance. Higher wage jobs are more likely to have access to employer-provided health insurance than lower wage jobs. As income rises, individuals are more likely to purchase health insurance because it is more affordable, because they have more assets to protect and because they are less likely to have access to free care in the event of an expensive medical outcome. Wages is the major component of income for some groups of tax filers while nonearned income (including self-employment income) is the major component for others. In the matching process, records within a cell were disaggregated into finer cells by the less important component of income and then were ranked by the more important component of income. Generally, tax-filing units categorized as employed and less than 65 years of age were ranked by wage, and the remaining units were ranked by nonwage income (including self-employed income).

For employed taxpayers under 65 years old, income is comprised mostly of wages. As a result, this group was first sub-divided by whether there was substantial nonwage income (including self-employed income) and then ranked by wage.[7] Specifically, the group was

---

[6] Tax-filing units with negative self-employment income were classified as wage earners or not employed depending on whether wages exceed the dollar threshold.

[7] For the CPS, the annual salary variable (or the hourly wage variable multiplied by the usual hours per week and weeks worked per year variables) was used to determine the annual wage.

sub-divided by whether nonwage income exceeded 10% of wages. Within each sub-division, the CPS record with the highest wage in a cell was matched to the record with the highest wage in the Panel model, and so forth.

For joint taxpayers the decision whether to purchase health insurance and in what combination depends on whether each spouse is working, whether one or both employers offer health insurance (correlated with each spouse's wage), and on total family income. In order to capture the essence of this complicated relationship, the group of joint taxpayers categorized as employed and under age 65 was subdivided by whether a female taxpayer worked, earned below the median of female taxpayers in the group, or earned above the median. Each of these three groups was further sub-divided by whether the combined nonwage income exceeded 10% of total wages. Then records within each of the six resulting sub-groups were ranked by the male's wage.[8]

Units categorized as not employed were ranked by total cash income.[9] This method of matching was also done in several situation where small cell sizes resulted in aggregation across employment categories (e.g., female taxpayers over 65 with children) and where wage breaks discussed below resulted in very small cells (e.g., self-employed joint taxpayers without children but with the male over 65 and the spouse under 65).

For the remaining units, units categorized as self-employed and units with taxpayers over age 65 (except as noted above), the initial methodology (breaking by nonwage income and ranking by wage) was reversed to reflect the fact that nonwage income is a more substantial component of total income for many units in these groups. These groups were generally sub-divided by wage(s) and then ranked by nonwage income (including self-employment income).

In the matching process, tax panel weights were used to determine the total population. CPS weights were used to construct the CPS file for the match but the match was not constrained to use all the CPS weighted observations. The weights on all CPS records in each cell were adjusted (pro rata) so that they summed to the total of the weights in the corresponding Panel Model cell.

CPS records could be split into two records as part of the matching process, but panel records were not split. When a CPS record was split into two or more records, the weight of the original record was split between the new records. If the combined weights of two or more (original or split) CPS records were required to equal the weight of a panel record, the CPS record in the group with the highest weight was matched to the panel record.

---

[8] Employed units with the male taxpayer over age 65 but with the spouse under age 65 (and no dependent children) were ranked in a similar manner.

[9] In the Panel, cash income includes wages, 401(K) contributions, taxable and nontaxable pension and annuity distributions, taxable IRA distributions, taxable and nontaxable Social Security income, taxable and tax exempt interest, dividends, self-employed income, other net income or loss, alimony, Veteran's benefits, welfare and other transfer payments, Supplemental Security Income, unemployment compensation in AGI, and worker's compensation. For purposes of matching only the income of the primary and secondary taxpayer were included in the total.

The match within a cell began by taking the top ranked record from each file and comparing their weights. Any left over weight from the adjusted CPS was compared with the second panel record. If the CPS weight was less than the panel weight, additional CPS records in the ranked order were processed until a match was completed. This process was continued until all the panel records in the cell were matched to a CPS record.

D. Initial and Subsequent Years

In the initial year, health insurance status was assigned as discussed below to each member of the tax unit. In subsequent years, tax-filing-units that did not have a life changing event kept the initial match and all the resulting health insurance statuses. Units that had a life changing event were re-matched to the CPS and may have had a change in health insurance statuses as a result. Life changing events include a change in family type or family composition (reflected in a change in person number), a change from dependent status to independent status, a change in employment type, a 15 percentile change in income, a 50 percent change in a filer's wage, or attainment of age 65 for at least one taxpayer. New entrants to the panel were matched in the year of entry.

E. Matching within the Unit

The CPS health insurance status and other variables for individuals within the unit were attached to Panel individuals following a set of rules. For single individuals, the CPS health variables were assigned to the panel observation. For married individuals, the CPS health variables of the male household head were assigned to the male taxpayer in the panel and the female household head were assigned to the female taxpayer. Depending on the kind of coverage, dependent coverage was assigned based on rules described below.

F. CPS Health Insurance Variables Carried to the Panel Model

The following describes how the CPS health insurance variables carried to the panel model were derived. One key measure of the impact of tax reform is the change in the number of uninsured individuals. The number of uninsured individuals is the residual of the total population less those individuals with identified coverage. Hence Medicare and Medicaid coverage status was included in the imputation along with employer-provided health insurance and nongroup coverage. Note the CPS health insurance status was for calendar year 2003.

Employer-Provided Health Insurance. Employer-provided health insurance included coverage from a current or former employer as well as Federal Tri-care coverage, including CHAMPUS, military, and Veterans benefits.[10] Dummy variables were created to indicate whether the coverage was single or family and whether the employer paid "all,

---

[10] CHAMPUS, military and Veterans benefits could not be separately distinguished.

part or none" of the premium[11] for each individual in the household. For individuals 65 years of age or older, employer-provided health insurance was categorized as primary[12] or secondary payer depending on whether the policyholder was working at the time of the survey. If any child in the CPS unit had employer coverage, then all children in the panel unit were assumed to have employer coverage.

Medicare. For individuals 65 years of age or older, dummy variables were created for whether Medicare was the primary or secondary payer. Dummy variables were also created for each household head under age 65 covered by Medicare due to disability.

Medicaid/SCHIP . The Medicaid/SCHIP population was divided into three groups: aged Medicaid participants; adult Medicaid participants or eligibles; and child Medicaid/SCHIP participants or eligibles. For filers, a dummy variable was created to indicate Medicaid coverage. In addition, an adult eligibility flag for Medicaid was created in the CPS file by randomly assigning eligibility based on AGI. If any child in the CPS unit was covered by Medicaid or SCHIP, all children eighteen years of age or younger were assigned Medicaid/SCHIP coverage in the panel unit. A child eligibility flag for Medicaid and SCHIP was also created in the CPS file by randomly assigning CPS units whose children were not covered by Medicaid, SCHIP or nongroup health insurance to the eligible category based on AGI. Flags were also created for SSI recipients to potentially identify units where at least one member may be disabled.

Nongroup Health Insurance. A dummy variable was created indicating nongroup coverage. As discussed above, the nongroup coverage variable was used to determine the self-employed with nongroup coverage cell. In addition, the nongroup dummy was carried to the panel for non-self-employed adults and their children under nineteen years old (or in school and less than 24 years of age.) Because families with several children may purchase nongroup coverage for only one child, if only one child in the CPS unit had nongroup health insurance, then only one child in the panel was randomly assigned nongroup health insurance. If more than one child in the CPS unit had nongroup health insurance, then all children in the panel unit were assigned nongroup health insurance.

Uninsured. Individuals without any identifiable health insurance were designated to be uninsured.

IV. Matching NHIS Nongroup Premiums to the Family Panel

NHIS single premiums were matched by: 3 age groups (older tax filer < 45; 45-54; 55-64); by 3 income groups (< $20,000; $20,000 - $75,000; $75,000+); and by gender of the policyholder. Within these cells, a hot-decking procedure was used to assign single

---

[11] The employer paid "all" category was assigned to individuals covered by Tri-care. Individuals with missing data, including individuals for whom the policyholder could not be identified, were assumed to receive a part contribution from their employer.

[12] Employer-provided health insurance was assumed to be primary and Medicare was assumed to be secondary if the policyholder was working even though in some cases the employer-provided health insurance may be secondary if the insurance was obtained from a former employer. If the policyholder was not working, Medicare was primary and employer-provided health insurance was secondary.

nongroup premiums to each tax-filing unit identified as having nongroup coverage on the family panel. In addition, childless couple premiums and family with children premiums were assigned to each tax-filing unit. The childless couple and couples with children premiums were calculated by multiplying the (male) single premium by the appropriate ratio below. These ratios were calculated from the NHIS data.

Ratio of family premiums to self-only by age and child status

	Age group			
	19-29	30-44	45-54	55-64
Couples without Children	1.34743	1.77032	1.84675	1.63109
Couples with Children	1.96309	2.25903	1.59680	1.70766

V. Matching MEPS Out-of-Pocket Medical Expenditures to the Family Panel

Out-of-pocket medical expenditures for individuals who had employer coverage for an entire year were used to impute out-of-pocket medical expenditures (including individuals without employer coverage) to individuals less than 65 years of age in the Panel Model.[13] Because medical expenses are heavily skewed, relatively few individuals with very high expenses account for a large portion of total spending, two years of data were combined to increase the sample size. Nonconsecutive years were used to avoid overweighting high cost medical events that begin in one year and end in the next. Expenses from 1996 and 1998 were indexed to 1997 to match the year of the data for employer premiums from the RWJF data.

Out-of-pocket expenses were matched by gender type and by five age groups (<19, 20-29, 30 - 39, 40 - 49, and 50 - 64). Within a gender/age cell, expenses were calculated at the following percentiles: (5, 10, 20, 30, 40, 50, 60, 70, 80, 90, 95, 99, 100th). Expenses were averaged between percentile breaks. Individual were randomly assigned a percentile and thus an expense amount.

VI. Health Insurance Variables Determined by Panel Data

The original tax panel provides data for three items. As previously mentioned, the self employed health insurance deduction provided nongroup insurance premiums for self-employed units claiming a self-employed health insurance deduction. Medical expenses that exceed 7 ½ % of AGI were in the panel data for itemizers. Finally, since virtually everyone over age 65 participates in Medicare, age from the family panel was used to assign Medicare for the aged.

---

[13] Including out-of-pocket medical expenses for individuals with employer-provided health insurance enables modeling of proposals that would provide a tax preference for or a cap on the combined value of premiums and out-of-pocket expenses.

APPENDIX C.4

Imputations: Transfer Income

by

James Cilke

and

Janet Holtzblatt

Transfer Income

I. Transfer Imputations

Transfers, such as social security and welfare benefits, represent income to recipients and thus should be included in a comprehensive measure of income.[1] To the extent that certain transfers are taxable, information on the incidence and the amount of transfers are available from tax returns and information returns. However, to a large extent, transfers are not taxable. We thus turn to other sources, including the Panel Survey on Income Dynamics, to impute nontaxable transfer income to the panel model. Using data from the National Income and Product Accounts (NIPA), targets were set for ten types of transfer income from 1987 through 1996. These are:

Fully taxable transfers
- Unemployment insurance

Partially taxable transfers
- Social security
- Tier 1 railroad retirement benefits ("social security equivalent benefits")

Nontaxable transfers
- Aid for Families with Dependent Children (AFDC)
- Food stamp benefits[2]
- Veterans cash benefits
- Supplemental Security Income (SSI)
- Low-income Home Energy Assistance Program (LIHEAP)
- Other cash public assistance (including general assistance and other state programs)
- Workers compensation

Beyond 1996, the transfers are extrapolated using information from both the NIPA and, to the extent that the transfers are federally funded, OMB's most recent budget forecast.

A. Fully Taxable Transfers: Unemployment insurance

Taxpayers must include total unemployment benefits in gross income. For filers, we used the reported amounts of unemployment benefits on the tax returns in the panel model. We compared these amounts with comparable information from the annual SOI Individual cross-section files. We found that unemployment benefits reported on the panel model were fairly consistent with the amounts reported on the SOI cross-section.

---

[1] Non-cash transfers are not included in our comprehensive definition of income due to difficulties in measuring their value. Examples of non-cash transfers include Medicare, Medicaid, school lunches, housing assistance, workers compensation health benefits, and veterans' education and health benefits.

[2] Strictly speaking, food stamps are not a cash transfer. Food stamp benefits are more fungible than other noncash transfers and are sometimes referred to as "near-cash" transfers. Thus, we include this benefit in our expanded income measure.

For non-filers, we used the amounts of unemployment compensation as reported on the PSID. We then compared the sum of unemployment benefits reported by filers and non-filers to the administrative targets. In each year, there was a shortfall. Since the panel model had tracked reasonably well the amounts reported by filers, the shortfall was made up by imputing unemployment benefits to non-filers.

To qualify for the imputed unemployment benefits, non-filers had to meet three criteria. First, they had to report earnings in the current or prior year. Second, they could not report unemployment benefits in the prior year. Third, the sum of AGI plus the imputed unemployment benefits had to be less than the filing threshold (otherwise, the unemployment benefits would have been taxable and reported on their tax returns). In addition, a fourth criteria applied to years other than 1987 (the first year of the panel) or 1992 and 1993 (years during which an economic downturn occurred). The fourth criterion was that earnings in the current year had to fall by more than ten percent from the prior year.

The amount of unemployment compensation imputed to non-filers was set equal to the average benefit received by non-filers with reported benefits and a decline in earnings.

B. Partially Taxable Transfers: Social Security and Tier 1 Railroad Retirement Benefits

Social security and Tier 1 railroad retirement benefits (which are equivalent to social security benefits) are partially taxable. Thus, some information about social security benefits is available from tax returns. Filers with taxable social security benefits report both the full amount and the taxable portion of social security benefits. In addition, the Social Security Administration and Railroad Retirement Board report social security and tier 1 railroad retirement benefits to individuals on SSA-1099s and RRB-1099s. For tax years 1989 and 1993 through 1996, we had a file that contained an exact match between the returns in the panel file and the SSA-1099s and RRB-1099s. For the non-filers, we used the amounts of social security benefits that they reported on the PSID.

Not surprisingly, the amount of social security reported on the panel model fell short of the targets based on administrative data. To make up for this shortfall, we imputed social security benefits to records without benefits in several stages.

First, we identified individuals who appeared to be missing social security benefits for some years (possibly because of the incomplete nature of the 1099 file). Beginning in 1988, benefits were imputed if an individual had reported benefits in year t-1 but did not report benefits in year t. The imputation was subject to two constraints:

- The social security earnings test (which phases-out benefits above an earnings threshold); and
- The income levels ("base amounts") at which a portion of social security benefits become taxable. Benefits were assumed to be zero if, when added to AGI, they would have been subject to the income tax and thus reported on tax returns.

The imputed benefit (prior to the imposition of the earnings test) was set equal to the benefit in year t, adjusted by the social security cost-of-living adjustment. We repeated this imputation methodology in reverse, starting in 1993.

Second, benefits for 1987 and 1988 were imputed to individuals who were deceased or did not file a return in 1989, did not have actual or imputed benefits in 1987 and 1988, and were at least 62 years of age. As in the first step, the imputation of benefits was subject to two constraints (the social security earnings test and the income thresholds for the taxation of benefits). In this stage, the imputed benefit (prior to the imposition of the earnings test) was set equal to $4,984 in 1987 and $5,180 in 1988.

Third, a very small amount of social security benefits was imputed to the panel model as part of the process of imputing filing returns.

In the fourth step, benefits were imputed for dependents of taxpayers within certain age groups who had not reported benefits. In 1996 only, the SOI file was matched to 1099s for dependents as well as the primary and secondary taxpayer. We used information from this matched file to calculate the selection probabilities for imputing social security benefits to dependents. These included:

- Dependent children on 1987 returns.
- Dependent children whose parent died sometime between 1987 and 1995. Benefits were imputed to the surviving children beginning in the year following the parent's death.
- Dependent children, between the ages of 2 and 18, who were claimed by a filer in any year between 1988 and 1996 but who were not previously claimed by the filer.
- Non-child dependents, aged 30 or older, on 1987 returns.
- Non-child dependent, aged 30 or older, who were claimed by a filer in any year between 1988 and 1996 but who were not previously claimed by the filer.

The imputed benefit was set equal to the average benefit for the year for other individuals in that age class (or half if the person died during the year).

To make up the remaining shortfalls in social security benefits on the panel model, we imputed benefits randomly to non-dependent filers who met the following criteria:

- For 1987 imputations: Earnings in 1987 and 1988 were below the point where the average benefit would be phased out by the social security earnings test, and their modified adjusted gross income was below the base amounts for taxation of social security benefits.
- For 1988 and later imputations: Same criteria as above but also restricted to individuals 55 and older

Aged-based probabilities were used in imputing benefits to non-dependent filers.

Finally, we imputed benefits to individuals who received social security benefits in year t-1 and year t+1 but not year t (subject to income tax and earnings test constraints described above). The imputed benefit was equal to the prior year social security benefit adjusted for inflation. If, however, the individual had earnings in excess of the earnings test threshold, then the imputed benefit was set equal to the person's maximum observed benefit in 1995 (adjusted by a deflator).

C. Non-taxable Transfers: Means-tested Transfers and Workers Compensation

Means-tested transfers are not taxable. These include
- Aid for Families with Dependent Children (AFDC) (since 1996, Temporary Assistance for Needy Families)
- Food stamp benefits
- Veterans cash benefits
- Supplemental Security Income (SSI)
- Low-income Home Energy Assistance Program (LIHEAP)
- Other cash public assistance (including general assistance and other state programs)

Thus, tax returns do not contain any information on the receipt of such public and private transfers. Workers compensation also is not taxable and thus not reported on tax returns.

To obtain information on non-taxable transfers, we performed an unconstrained statistical match between the panel and the constructed PSID panel file. The PSID asks individuals about the receipt of AFDC, veterans cash benefits, SSI, other cash public assistance, and workers compensation.[3] In addition, the PSID asks families about their receipt of food stamp benefits and LIHEAP. Prior to the match, we aggregated transfer income at the family level for all items.

The statistical match employed a penalty function where, in each year, every tax family on the panel was compared with every tax filing unit on the constructed PSID file. The PSID record with the lowest penalty was the matching record.

The filing units were matched based on demographic characteristics, including:
- family status;
- age;
- number of dependents; and
- whether the primary taxpayer or his or her spouse had died in the current or following year.

In addition, the filing units were matched based by the filing unit's relative income ranking (using modified adjusted gross income) and the presence and amount of certain types of income (investment income, social security, taxable pensions, and

---

[3] More detailed information is available for the head of the household and his or her spouse than for other family members in the household.

unemployment compensation). Finally, for years after 1987, filing units were matched based on the presence of certain types of transfer income in the prior year.

During the match, penalties were assigned when discrepancies in the income and demographic variables occurred between the PSID constructed panel file and the tax panel. Transfer income is generally underreported in household surveys like the PSID. To help compensate for such shortfalls, we gave a bonus to potential matches reporting transfer income. Further, for certain types of transfers, we assumed that families generally continue to receive that type of transfer year after year. Under this assumption, we penalized potential matches to PSID records with certain types of transfer income if that type of transfer income was not reported in the prior year.

After the match was completed, we adjusted the means-tested transfer amounts on the panel model to hit targets based on the administrative data. We also eliminated means-tested benefits for filing units with adjusted gross income in excess of $50,000 (1987 dollars).

We then compared the totals for workers compensation on the panel model to the administrative data targets. The administrative data targets included both public (federal employee, state programs, and black lung) and private forms of workers compensation. However, we observed that the amounts of workers compensation on the panel model fall greatly short of the administrative data targets. Speculating that some workers compensation was reported in the PSID as "other transfers," we designated a portion of this miscellaneous account as workers compensation for returns without such benefits. Even after this imputation step, the amounts of workers compensation on the panel model fell short of the targets. We next determined the probability of receiving workers compensation based on family and income characteristics. Using these probabilities, we then imputed workers compensation to other returns without such benefits.

After matching the aggregate targets for the non-taxable transfers, we then compared average benefits on the Panel Model with estimated average benefits based on administrative data. If the averages on the panel model exceeded the administrative averages by more than ten percent, we reallocated transfer income. First, we imputed transfer income to certain low-income returns without any transfer income. Then, to ensure that we still met the aggregate targets, we reduced proportionately all the imputed transfer amounts.

II. Transfer Targets and Extrapolation

As noted above, we compared the amounts of transfer income on the panel model to administrative data targets. Through 2002, the targets for federal and state transfers were derived from the National Income Products and Accounts (NIPA) Table 3.12 ("Government Social Benefits"). Data on workers compensation paid by private funds came from NIPA Table 6.11C ("Employer Contributions for Employee Pension and Insurance Funds by Industry and by Type"). An adjustment was made to the NIPA target for social security benefits to take out the portion of benefits received by the institutionalized population (who are not included in the panel model).

Beginning in 2003, the targets for federally-funded transfers are based on OMB projections for the most recent President's budget. OMB provides these data on a fiscal year basis, which we adjust to a calendar year basis. For non-federally-funded transfers, the most recent NIPA data are adjusted for projected changes in the consumer price index (as estimated in the most recent President's budget).

In some instances, we also compared the average transfer amount received by filing units on the panel model to administrative data. Our sources for the number of recipients included the Social Security Bulletin Annual Statistical Supplement or the Statistical Abstract of the United States. In some instances, information on the number of recipients was available only for specific points-in-time (typical month), and it was necessary to estimate the total number of recipients throughout the year.

APPENDIX D.1

Extrapolation: Notes

by

James Cilke

Notes

I. Overview

Aging or extrapolating the panel model is a multi-staged process. Fundamentally, we will extrapolate the first year of the panel (1987 records) to the first year of our budget cycle (currently 2004). We will accomplish this by first extrapolating 1987 records to 1996 levels using a complicated semi-constrained statistical match. The relative growth from 1987 to 1996 will be applied to all records in the file. Thus, as a result of the match, 1995 records will be aged to 2004 levels. The, next step will be to repeat the process with a statistical match between 1987 records and 1995-extrapolated-to-2004 records.

The basic strategy under the first semi-constrained match is to link a non-dependent 1987 return (filer and non-filer) with a non-dependent 1996 "Cross-section" return. The dollar values on the 87 return will be adjusted by a series of growth factors so that total income on the 87 return equals the matched 96 return. Weights on 87 returns will be adjusted so that the weighted number of 1987 returns within a matching cell equals the weighted number of 1996 returns in the same cell.

Initially, the same dollar-adjustment factors applied to a panel member's 1987 return will be applied to all future years in the panel. Thus, the relationship between dollar items across years for a panel member will remain unchanged. For example, if wages on the panel member's 1988 return is twice the amount on his 1987 return, then the extrapolated 1997 return will, initially, have twice the wages as the extrapolated 1996 return.

However, the extrapolated file may not hit known or predicted targets for certain sources of income or types of itemized deductions. So, as a final step, income and deduction items will be uniformly adjusted to hit target amounts.

II. Income Sources for Defining the Income Type Cell

The first step was to collapse the various sources of income into separate categories. These categories are used to classify returns by their type of income.

1. Wage income: (wages plus unemployment compensation less IRA contributions and the foreign earned income exclusion).
2. Investment income: (interest, dividends, capital gains in AGI, and supplemental gains in AGI).
3. Retirement income: (taxable pensions, taxable IRA distributions, and Social Security benefits).
4. Business income: (positive amounts of income included in AGI from sole proprietors, partners, SBCs, and rents).
5. Business losses: (amounts of losses which reduce AGI from sole proprietors, partners, SBCs, rents, and NOLS)
6. Other income: (all other positive amounts of income included in AGI).

7. Other losses: (all other negative income amounts that reduce AGI and all non-business related adjustments to AGI (e.g., alimony paid, penalty on early withdrawal of savings, and the foreign housing exclusion.)
8. Non-taxable transfers income: (The sum of non-taxable transfers imputed to the panel model.)
9. Other non-taxable incomes: (Tax exempt interest and non-taxable pensions to the extent that the non-taxable portion is less than the taxable portion.)

Passive losses allowed from the phase-in rule occurred in 1987 but not 1996. Thus, to make the income measures comparable, I disallow any passive losses allowed under the phase-in rule. This step either raises business income in 4 or lowers business losses in 5.

For filers, the total target income (or matching income) is the sum of the first 7 income types. For a return, this sum can be described as AGI plus non-taxable Social Security benefits plus those business adjustments that otherwise reduce AGI. For non-filers, the total target income is the sum of all 9 income categories

III. Defining the Super Matching Cells

The next step is to place the 87 and 96 returns into "super" matching cells. The super matching cells are defined as follows.

A) Marital status (ISTAT):
    1 = Singles and MFS returns
    2 = Joints
    3 = Head-of-house and Widower returns

B) Age of primary class (IAGECL):
    1 = Under 40 years
    2 = 40 to 59 years
    3 = 60 years and up

C) Gender (for ISTAT=1 or ISTAT=3) (ISEX):
    1 = Male
    2 = Female

D) Two-earner indicator (for ISTAT=2) (ITWO):
    1 = 0 or 1-earner couple
    2 = 2-earner couple

E) Number of dependents) (IDEP_NO):
    1 = zero
    2 = One
    3 = Two or more.

F) Filer status (IFILST):

1 = Non-filer or filer with zero AGI and zero Social Security benefits.
2 = Filer

G) Income type (INC_TYPE):
1 = Wage income is over 90% of total targeted income and total losses from all sources is less than $3001.
2 = Capital gains is over $3000 and capital gains is over 25% of total targeted income, or, investment income (dividends, interest, and capital gains) is over 50% of total targeted income.
3 = Positive business income is over 50% of total targeted income.
4 = Retirement income is over 50% of total targeted income.
5 = Total targeted income is zero or less (regardless of the above assignments).
6 = Everybody else.

IV. Collapsing Thin Cells

Categorizing returns with these cell definitions created a number of "thin" cells. In other cases, the number of sample observations within a cell was sufficient. However, there was a wide disparity between the weighted number of returns in the 87-cell compared with the similarly-defined 96-cell. So, the next step was to eliminate certain cell boundaries. I applied the following rules to collapse the cells. For non-filers (IFILST=0), I eliminated the two-earner distinction, the number of dependents distinction, and the age class distinction. In addition, for joint non-filers, I eliminated the income type distinction. Further, for head-of-household non-filers, I eliminated the gender distinction.

For filing singles, I eliminated the two-earner distinction and the number of dependents distinction. For filing joints, I eliminated the gender distinction. I also eliminated the two-earner distinction for joints where the dominate source of income was investment income or retirement income (INC_TYPE=2 or INC_TYPE=4). For elderly joints, I eliminated the number of dependents distinction.

For head-of-household and widower returns, I eliminated the number of children distinction. Further, if the income type was the catch-all category (INC_TYPE=6), then I eliminated the age distinction and the gender distinction. Finally, if the head-of-house or widower was elderly, I eliminated the number of dependents distinction.

In the end, the matching procedure formed 121 super matching cells.

V. Determining Income Growth Rates within Super-Cells

At this point, each 1987 record is placed into one (and only one) 87-level super-cell, and each 1996 record is placed into one 96-level super-cell. Within each super-cell, and for each file, I calculated the average level of each income source. The average only includes those records with that particular income source. That is, I calculated average incomes for:

01)   Wages,
02)   Unemployment compensation,
03)   Interest,
04)   Dividends,
05)   Capital gains,
06)   Income from Sole Proprietors and farms,
07)   Income from partnerships, SBCs, and rents plus royalties,
08)   Losses from partnerships, SBCs, and rents plus royalties,
09)   Income from taxable pensions and taxable IRA distributions,
10)   Social Security benefits,
11)   Other incomes,
12)   Other losses,
13)   Total targeted income,
14)   Total targeted income less capital gains,
15)   Total non-taxable transfers income
16)   AFDC Transfers income
17)   Supplemental Security income
18)   Veteran's cash benefits
19)   Workers compensation benefits,
20)   Food Stamps
21)   Other Welfare payments
22)   Other transfer income

Now then, for each income source and within each super-cell, dividing the 1996 average by the 1987 average yields a growth rate factor. These growth factors will be used later on to grow a 1987 record to 1996 levels.[1]

VI. Defining Income Sub-Matching Cells – on 1996 Records

At this point, I have the 1996 records within a super-cell sorted by total income. I also know the weighted number of records within each super-cell. The next step is divide the super matching cells into roughly equally-sized sub-matching cells. By equally-sized, I mean that the weighted number of returns within each sub-cell of a given super-cell will be approximately the same. The sub-cell boundaries are to be determined by age and total income quantiles. Our goal is to put at least 20 unweighted observations in each sub-cell. However, we would accept cells with 10 or more observations.

The first step was to determine the sub-cell breaks based on income. Observations within each super-cell were sorted, highest to lowest, by total income. Next, for each super-cell, I compared the number of observations within similarly-defined super-cells in the 87 and 96 files; the minimum of these two values would be used to determine the initial number of income breaks. The following table shows the initial number of income classes the super-cell would be divided into:

---

[1] The adjustment factors are capped at 4.0 and 0.25.

Min number of observations 87 vs. 96	Initial number of Income classes
-------------	-------------
2000 and up	10
1620 - 1999	09
1280 - 1619	08
980 - 1279	07
720 - 979	06
500 - 719	05
320 - 499	04
180 - 319	03
80 - 179	02
Under 80	01

Say that, based on the above step, I will divide a given super-cell into 5 sub-cells. I would take the top $1/5^{th}$ (20%) of the <u>weighted number</u> of records within each 1996 super-cell and assign them a code indicating they are in the top sub-cell within the super-cell. Finally, I would note and save the income value of the last record placed in the cell.

As a general rule, the higher a return's income, the lower the weight on the return is likely to be. So, given the above procedure and example, it is likely that more the $1/5^{th}$ of the <u>sample number</u> of records were placed in the highest income sub-cell. So, at this point, I re-determine the number of additional income-derived sub-cells.

Here,

$87adj = N^i_{87} * (1. - (a^i_{96} / N^i_{96}))$, and
$96adj = N^i_{96} - a^i_{96}$

where N^i_{87} and N^i_{96} are the original sample number of records in the with 1987 and 1996 super-cells, and a^i_{96} is the sample number of these records going into the top income sub-cell. I then use the following table to determine the number of additional income sub-cells (up to a maximum of 9) I will create. The row is determined by the minimum of 87adj and 96adj.

Min number of observations 87adj vs. 96adj	Additional number of Income classes
-------------	-------------
1740 and up	09
1360 - 1739	08
1020 – 1359	07
760 - 1019	06
540 - 759	05
360 - 539	04
220 - 359	03
100 - 219	02
Under 100	01

Continuing with my example, say I have enough remaining observations in the super-cell to create 4 additional sub-cells. I have already sorted observations by income and put those observations with the highest income in the first income sub-cell. So, the second income sub-cell is filled with the next 25% of the remaining <u>weighted</u> observations. The third income sub-cell is filled with the next 25%, and so on until all observations within any given super-cell are placed in an income-based sub-cell. Again, I note the level of total income received by the last return in the sub-cell.

VII. Defining Income Sub-Matching Cells – on 1987 Records

At this point, every 1996 record is a member of one and only one income-defined sub-cell. In the next step, I put 1987 records into equally-defined sub-cells. First, I "extrapolate" each 1987 record by the series of growth factors described above. That is, the wages on each 1987 return within a super-cell are adjusted by the average per-capita change in wages in that super-cell between 1987 and 1996. Similarly, unemployment benefits are adjusted by the unemployment growth factor, interest income is adjusted by the interest income growth factor, and so on.[2] The individual income components are then summed to create an extrapolated total income. Finally, each 1987 observation is placed into one income-defined sub-cell according to the same income breaks used to define the sub-cells on 1996 records.

VIII. Defining Age Sub-Matching Cells

In the next step, I divide each of the income-defined sub-cells into finer sub-cells that are defined by age breaks. Starting with the 96 file, I sort the observations by age within each income-define sub-cell. (I added a random univariate number between 0 and 1 to everybody's age to assist in rank-ordering observations with equal ages.) Next, I compared the number of observations within similarly-defined sub-cells in the 87 and 96

---

[2] In this step, incomes from transfer payments except Social Security and Unemployment Compensation are adjusted by the growth factor for total transfers income. I will use the growth factors for specific transfer sources later on. Similarly, at this stage, I do not use the "Total Income except Gains" growth factor.

files; the minimum of these two values would be used to determine the number of age breaks. The following table shows the number of age classes the sub-cell would be divided into:

Min number of observations in a sub-cell 87 vs. 96	Number of Age classes
200 and up	10
180 - 199	09
160 - 179	08
140 - 159	07
120 - 139	06
100 - 119	05
80 - 99	04
60 - 79	03
20 - 59	02
Under 20	01

For example, say a given income-defined sub-cell can be divided into 4 age-defined sub-cells. I would take the youngest 1/4th of the records within that sub-cell and assign them a code indicating they are in the first age-defined sub-cell. Additionally, I would note and save the age value of the last record placed in the cell. I would then use these same age breaks to assign 87 records into age-defined sub-cells.

IX. Collapsing Thin Cells

The just described puts each 1987 and 1996 tax record into a unique matching sub-cell. Unfortunately, the procedure allowed for the possibility that the number of observations within the sub-cell is too thin (e.g., under 10 observations). Recall that the income breaks and age breaks used to define the sub-cells on the 87 file came from breaks which were designed to evenly allocate records on the 96 file.

So, I began by finding those matching sub-cells on the 87 file that had less than 10 observations. If so, I merged the cell with an adjoining cell with higher income. For example, if I divided a super-cell into 5 income-defined sub-cells and the third sub-cell, on the 87 file, had less than 10 observations, I simply joined the third cell with the second cell. To keep the cell definitions consistent, I merged the same two cells on the 96 file. Next I repeated this same procedure to catch the rare cases where a combined sub-cell still had less than 10 observations. Next, I repeated this same procedure except that I joined those top income sub-cells containing less than 10 observations with an adjoining sub-cell with less income. Finally, in the case where a super-cell was divided into two age-defined sub-cells and one of the sub-cells had less than 10 observations, I merged the two sub-cells into a single matching cell. As a final step, I sort-ordered the records in each cell by total income (highest to lowest).

X. Reweighting Each 87 Record

To summarize, each 1987 record and each 1996 record are placed into a uniquely-defined matching cell. Each matching cell is defined as a super-cell that is further divided into sub-cells or matching cells based on the income and age of each record. For each matching cell for 1996 records, there is a corresponding (identically identified) matching cell for 1987 records. The next step is to uniformly adjust the return weights of each 1987 record such that the sum of the weights in the matching cell equals the sum of the weights in the corresponding 1996 matching cell. Thus, after all 87 weights are adjusted, the weighted sum of all 1987 records will equal the weighted sum of all 1996 records.

XI. Reallocate 1987 Returns into Sub-Cells All Over Again

Recall from above that each super-cell is divided into a number of sub-cells based on the sample number of returns within the super-cell. So for example, if I decided to divide a super-cell into 5 income sub-cells, I would place approximately $1/5^{th}$ of the weighted number of returns within the super-cell into each sub-cell. In the case of 1987 returns, I used the original 1987 weights.

We then decided that it would be more appropriate if we filled sub-cells of 1987 records using each 1987 record's adjusted weight. So, I repeated the process of filling 1987 records into sub-cells. That is, I repeated the statistical matching process beginning after the point where I determined each sub-cell's income break points. The end result is that some 1987 records were placed in a different matching sub-cell. (We could have repeated the process a third time. However, we assumed that greatest benefit from this iterative process would come in the first step.)

XII. The Match

At this point, I was ready to do the actual statistical match. Working, within each matching cell, I linked the top record with the 1987 cell to the top record in the 1996 cell. The weight on this matched record is the minimum of the 1996 record's weight or the 1987 record's adjusted weight. If the 1987 record had the greater weight, I would then match the same 1987 record a second time to the next 1996 record. This time, however the record weight of the 1987 record would be reduced by that minimum weight from the previous match. Again, the weight of this matched record would be the minimum of the two record weights. I would continue matching the 1987 record until his record weight was completely exhausted. Similarly, a 1996 record would be matched multiple times if it had the larger weight in its first match. Recall that, by design, the sum of the weights of the 1987 records in the matching cell exactly equaled the sum of the weights of the 1996 records. At the end of this step, every 1987 record is linked to one or more 1996 records. Interestingly, the only information from the 1996 record that it kept is the 1996 record's total income amount.

XIII. Blowing Up Dollar Values From 1987 to 1996 Levels

At this point in the process I am ready to begin adjusting the exogenous dollar values on the now-split 1987 returns. I start by hitting each dollar value by one of the super-cell growth factors (described above). In effect, for income items, I repeat the process used in the matching process (described above) of growing 1987 total income to 1996 levels.[3] However, I apply a growth factor to all exogenous dollar items including credits and itemized deductions. Non-income items are adjusted by either the Total Income growth factor, or the Total-Income-Except-Gains growth factor.

After adjusting all dollar amounts, I then recalculate total income. I then compare this amount to the 1996 total income amount derived from the statistical match. For each micro-record, I calculate the ratio of the statistically matched 1996 value and the 87-now-96 total income value. This ratio becomes a second dollar adjustment factor and is applied to all exogenous dollar values.[4]

Next, I hit each income item with an across-the-board factor such that the weighted sum of that income hits the weighted sum found on original 96 returns. For example, after adjusting wages on each return by the super-cell growth factor and further adjusting wages by the micro-level statistical match factor, I discovered that total wages on 87-now-96 returns was slightly (1.9%) short of the original amount of total wages on original 96 returns. So, I bumped up wages on every return by 1.9% such that wages on the 87-now-96 returns equals wages on the original 96 returns. I performed a similar procedure for the remaining income items with targets. The following table enumerates the specific income targets

Wages (in AGI)
Tax exempt interest
Taxable interest
Dividends
Taxable Pensions and IRA distributions
Capital Gains in AGI
Schedule C Income
Schedule C losses
Schedule E Partnership income
Schedule E Partnership losses
Schedule E SBC income
Schedule E SBC losses
Schedule E Rental income

---

[3] This time, however, each transfer income item is grown by its own super-cell growth factor. Further, for returns with total positive income, loss items are not allowed to grow beyond their initial levels. Similarly, for returns with net losses, the growth factors for positive income items are capped at 1.0.

[4] If the 87-now-96 record contains and IRA adjustment, both the numerator (target-96 value) and denominator (extrapolated 96 value) are reduced by the IRA adjustment. Further, if capital gains on the 87-now-96 record is exactly at the loss limit (i.e., -3000 or −1500 for MFS) then gains are removed from the calculated ratio. The ratio of the target 1996 value over the 87-now-96 value is capped at 10.0 and 0.10. Finally, I set the ratio to 1.00 in the rare cases where the target 96 value has a different sign than the extrapolated 96 value.

Schedule E Rental losses
Schedule F Farm income
Schedule F Farm losses
Social Security (and Railroad Retirement) benefits
Unemployment compensation
All other income included in AGI
All other losses included in AGI
AFDC/TANF benefits
Other welfare benefits
Veterans cash benefits
Supplemental Security income
Workman's compensation (cash) benefits
Food stamps

As part of this last step, I calculate, for each record, the change in total income and the change in total income without gains. For example, say the cumulative effect on a return of adjusting each income item is to raise total income (and total income without gains) by 2%. I would then raise certain non-income items (e.g., itemized deductions) by 2%. Most non-income items are hit by the income-without-gains factor. Non-income items hit by the total income factor include charitable contributions, investment interest expenses, and state and local income taxes.

Not too surprisingly, total values for itemized deductions on 87-now-96 returns drifted from those values on the original 1996 returns. To correct, I applied a set of across-the-board adjustment factors to selected itemized deduction amounts. In particular, I hit targets for charitable contributions, home mortgage interest expenses, investment interest expenses, state and local income taxes, state and local property taxes, medical expenses, and miscellaneous expenses. (About the only exogenous non-income values that were not specifically targeted relate to personal and business credits.)

To summarize this step, each exogenous dollar value on each non-dependent 1987 return is blown up by a series of adjustment factors. The first factor is the average growth of some item within a super matching cell. The second factor is a micro-level factor applied to all exogenous values and is designed to adjust total income on the 1987 return to hit the total income amount that was on the matching 1996 return. The third factor is applied to income items such that the weighted sum of each specific income item hits the known 1996 totals for that item. For non-income items, the third factor is equal to the combined affect on total income or total income without gains. The fourth factor, applied to itemized deductions only, adjusts deductions such that the weighted sum of the deduction for itemizers hits the known 1996 amounts.

XIV. Extrapolating Beyond 1996

Once the set of adjustment factors for aging a 1987 non-dependent return to 1996 levels are established, aging any subsequent return falls easily into place. Each person's subsequent returns, from 1988 to 1996, are first adjusted by the same set of adjustment factors used on the 1987 return. So, 1998 returns are aged to 1997 levels, 1989 returns to 1998 levels, and so on. Then, to control for any drift, each specific income item is hit with and single adjustment factor such that the weighted sum of that income item hits the known or target amount for that item. Note that the targets for 1998, 1999, and 2000 levels are obtained from tabulations from the Individual SOI files for those years. For years 2001 and beyond, the targets, in general, are the same as used to extrapolate OTA's Individual Tax Model. In both cases, the targets are for tax filers only. So, before applying the income-specific factors, I first must assign a filer/non-filer status variable to each return.

Initially, any return that was actually filed and processed by SOI is treated as a "filing" return in an extrapolated year. In addition, any return with income included in AGI that is above the filing threshold or any return with a non-zero tax liability is treated as a filer. The filing threshold for any return is simply the sum of the personal exemptions for primary taxpayer (and spouse if joint) plus the standard deduction, including any additional amounts for being over 64 years of age and/or being blind. I then compare this count of filers with the target number of returns. If I need additional returns, I first begin by converting non-filers with the highest AGIs into filers. If possible, I convert just enough non-filers so that the total number of filers hits the target number. If, after exhausting the pool of non-filers with positive AGI, I am still short of filers, I will then randomly convert non-filers with zero AGI into filers. Conversely, if I initially have too many filers, I will convert those filers without liability and with income below the filing threshold into non-filers. I start by randomly selecting returns without earned income to become a non-filer.

With the filer/non-filer flag in hand, I can then compare income totals on extrapolated panel returns with targeted amounts. Note that once I determine an adjustment factor for a given income source, I will apply that factor to all returns, both filers and non-filers. This may cause some non-filers to switch to filers. So, the process of determining an income adjustment factor is an iterative one.

APPENDIX D.2

Extrapolation: Algebraic Description

by

James R. Nunns

Algebraic Description

This paper provides a step-by-step algebraic description of the first extrapolation of the panel from the historic 1987-1996 period to the 1996-2005 period. The second extrapolation of the panel, to the 2004-2013 period (the "04 budget period"), is nearly identical to the first extrapolation so is not described separately. However, the descriptions of steps in the first extrapolation include notes explaining any differences in the second extrapolation. The paper includes references to the spreadsheets used to develop the target levels or growth rates used in the extrapolations.

This paper does not describe the formation of super-cells, the formation of income and age quantiles within super-cells, reweighting records, or the micro-level record match (which results in record splitting). These are all described in detail in Jim Cilke's "Panel Extrapolation Notes."

The paper is divided into three sections. Section I describes the extrapolation of 1997 returns[1] to 1996 levels. Section II describes the remainder of the first extrapolation, of 1988-1996 returns to 1997-2005 levels. Section III provides documentation for the targets used in the extrapolations.

I. Extrapolation of 1987 Returns to 1996 Levels

It is assumed that all non-dependent returns in the 1987 and 1996 files have been placed in corresponding super-cells (with certain super-cells collapsed[2]) and placed in corresponding income and age quantiles within super-cells (with certain quantiles collapsed[3]), the weights of all 1987 returns in each super-cell have been adjusted proportionately so that the weighted number of returns matched the weighted number of returns in the corresponding 1996 super-cell, and the micro-level record match (with record splitting) to have already taken place. Note that the record match involves adjustments to the income on 1987 returns that is nearly identical to Steps 1-3 described below.

Steps 1 and 2 adjust the average income from each income source on 1987 returns to the average for 1996 returns in the same super-cell.

---

[1] Throughout, the term "return" is used to describe the basic units used in the extrapolations, which for filers are income tax returns and for non-filers are the unit that would have been used for filing an income tax return. Unless otherwise noted, only non-dependent return units are used in computing the factors used in the extrapolation.

[2] Super-cells were collapsed if they contained too few observations (unweighted returns) in the cell, or if the weighted number of observations in the 1987 and corresponding 1996 cell were too disparate. See "Panel Extrapolation Notes" for a description of the specific super-cells that were collapsed.

[3] Income and age quantiles were collapsed into surrounding quantiles if there were too few (generally, defined as less than 10) observations in the 1987 super-cell. See "Panel Extrapolation Notes."

In these and subsequent steps, upper-case variables (such as Y_j for income from source j) denote weighted amounts for a group (or all) returns, whereas lower-case variables (such as y_{ij} for income from source j on return i) denote unweighted return-level amounts or scalars (such as a_j^S which is defined in Step 1).

<u>Step 1</u>

Compute for each income item j in each super-cell S the ratio a_j^S where:

$$a_j^S = (Y_j^{S96} / N_j^{S96})/(Y_j^{S87} / N_j^{S87})$$

and Y_j^{St} is aggregate of income from source j in super-cell S in year t

     N_j^{St} is the number of returns with income from source j in super-cell S in year t

Note that the a_j^S ratios are capped at 4.0 and 0.25.

Note also that somewhat different groupings of income sources are used in defining the a_j^S ratios than are used in defining the c_j ratios in Step 7, below. (See Jim Cilke's "Panel Extrapolation Notes.")

<u>Step 2</u>

Apply a_j^S to income item j on 1987 return i (in super-cell S).

$$y_{ij}^{87E1} = a_j^S \, y_{ij}^{87}$$

where y_{ij} is income from source j for return i

and   87E1 denotes the first stage of the extrapolation of 1987 to 1996

Note that a_j^S applies to any return filed by a dependent on return i.

Steps 3-5 adjust the total income on each 1987 return to the total income on the matched 1996 return.

Step 3

Compute a new total income for each 1987 return i: $y_i^{87E1} = \sum_j y_{ij}^{87E1}$

Note that for filers total income omits all non-taxable sources of income except non-taxable social security benefits.

Note also that if the sign on total income on a return was switched by the application of the a_j^S factors, the a_j^S factors were set to 1.0 for all loss items on that return (if the return initially had positive total income) or for all positive items (if the return initially had negative total income) and total income was recomputed.[1]

Step 4

Compute for each 1987 return i the ratio b_i where:

$b_i = y_i^{96} / y_i^{87E1}$ where y_i^{96} is the total income on the 1996 return matched to 1987 return i

Note that IRA contributions at the contribution limit and capital losses at the loss limit were not included in y_i^{96} or y_i^{87E1} for this computation. Further, b_i was capped at 10.0 and 0.1 and set to 1.0 if the signs of y_i^{96} and y_i^{87E1} were different.

Step 5

Apply b_i to all income items of unit i as adjusted in Step 2 to give the second stage of the 1987 extrapolation to 1996:

$$y_{ij}^{87E2} = b_i \, y_{ij}^{87E1}$$

Note that b_i applies to any return filed by a dependent on return i.

Steps 6-8 adjust aggregate income from each source on all returns from Step 5 to actuals for 1996. (For the years 2001 and later of the first extrapolation, described in Section II, and for the second extrapolation, forecasts would be used in Step 7.)

Step 6

---

[1] It is unclear from "Panel Extrapolation Notes" what, if anything, was done if the sign on total income remained switched.

Compute for all returns (including dependents' returns) the sum of each income item j as adjusted in Step 5:

$$Y_j^{87E2} = \sum_i Y_{ij}^{87E2} \qquad \text{where} \quad Y_{ij}^{87E2} \text{ is the weighted amount of}$$

$$y_{ij}^{87E2}$$

Note that for taxable income items, the sum is computed only for filers, since the actuals (or forecast targets) are only for filers (see Step 7).

Step 7

Compute the ratio c_j for each income item j where:

$$c_j = Y_j^{87T}/Y_j^{87E2} \qquad \text{where} \quad Y_j^{87T} \text{ is the actual (or forecast target)}$$
$$\text{for } Y_j \text{ in 1996 (2001 and later)}$$

Note that for taxable income items the ratio is computed only for filers, since the actuals (or forecast targets) are only for filers.

Step 8

Apply c_j to income item j, as adjusted in Step 5, on all returns (filer, including dependent, and non-filer) to give the third stage of the extrapolation of 1987 returns to 1996 levels. This is the final stage of the first extrapolation for income items.

$$y_{ij}^{87E3} = c_j \, y_{ij}^{87E2} = c_j \, b_i \, a_j^S \, y_{ij}^{87}$$

Steps 9-11 apply the income adjustment factors from the preceding steps to non-income items that are "exogenous" (i.e., are not determined from other items on a return). Non-income items include some adjustments to income, itemized deductions, certain credit amounts (e.g., child care expenses for the CDCTC, the amount of the general business credit), AMT timing preferences, and non-taxable IRA and pension distributions. These items are quite similar to the non-income items that are grown by Stage 1 per capita growth factors in the extrapolation of the ITM, but Jim Cilke's code needs to be consulted to determine exactly which items are included.

Step 9

Compute the total income, and total income without capital gains, as adjusted through Step 8 on each 1987 return i:

$$y_i^{87E3} = \sum_j y_{ij}^{87E3}$$

and

$$(y_i^{87E3} - y_{ig}^{87E3}) \qquad\qquad \text{where} \quad y_{ig}^{87E3} \text{ is capital gains on return } i$$

<u>Step 10</u>

Compute the ratio of total income, with and without capital gains, from Step 9 to the original amounts for 1987 on each 1987 return i:

$$d_i^W = y_i^{87E3} / y_i^{87}$$

and

$$d_i^{WO} = (y_i^{87E3} - y_{ig}^{87E3})/(y_i^{87} - y_{ig}^{87})$$

<u>Step 11</u>

Apply d_i^W to charitable contributions, investment interest expense, and state and local income taxes (items denoted with the subscript k in the following steps) on all returns i in 1987 (that have itemized deductions);

Apply d_i^{WO} to all other exogenous non-income items (those denoted with the subscript l in the following steps) on all returns i in 1987.

Application of these factors brings exogenous non-income items up to the third stage of the extrapolation of 1987 returns to 1996 levels.

$$x_{ik}^{87E3} = d_i^W x_{ik}^{87} \qquad\qquad \text{where} \quad x_{ik}^t \text{ is the amount of non-income item } k \text{ on return } i \text{ in year (actual or extrapolated) } t$$

and

$$x_{il}^{87E3} = d_i^{WO} x_{il}^{87} \qquad\qquad \text{where} \quad x_{il}^t \text{ is the amount of non-income item } l \text{ on return } i \text{ in year}$$

Steps 12-14 adjust the aggregate amounts of certain (targeted) itemized deductions[1] on all returns from Step 11 for differential rates of growth of these deductions <u>relative to</u> the forecast growth rates for total income or total income without capital gains. For 1996-2000, actual levels of the factors used for itemized deductions and of total income with and without capital gains were used in computing relative growth rates. For 2001 and later, forecasts were used. The method of computing rates of growth is described in Section III of the paper.

<u>Step 12</u>

Compute the per capita growth rates of total income and total income without capital gains and the per capita growth rates for the targeted itemized deductions. Note that since only filers have itemized deductions, total income is as defined for filers.

$$r_Y = (Y^t / N^t)/(Y^{t-1} / N^{t-1})$$

$$r_{Y-G} = ((Y^t - Y_g^t)/N^t)/((Y^{t-1} - Y_g^{t-1})/ N^{t-1})$$

r_k = the per capita growth rate computed from Budget forecast variables for targeted itemized deduction k (see Section III of the paper)

r_l = the per capita growth rate computed from Budget forecast variables for targeted itemized deduction l (see Section III of the paper).

<u>Step 13</u>

Compute the ratio e_k or e_l for each targeted itemized deduction k or l:

$$e_k = r_k / r_Y$$

$$e_l = r_l / r_{Y-G}$$

<u>Step 14</u>

Apply e_k (e_l) to itemized deductions k (l), as adjusted in Step 13 of all returns i in 1987. This is the fourth, and final, stage of the extrapolation for these itemized deductions.

---

[1] The specific itemized deductions adjusted in Steps 12-14 are: charitable contributions, investment interest expense, and state and local income taxes (items denoted with the subscript k) and home mortgage interest expense, state and local property taxes, and medical expenses (items denoted with the subscript l).

$$x_{ik} = e_k \, x_{ik}^{87E3}$$

$$x_{il} = e_l \, x_{il}^{87E3}$$

With the re-computation of endogenous variables, those computed from other (now extrapolated) variables on the return, the extrapolation of 1987 returns to 1996 levels is complete.

II. Extrapolation of 1988-1996 Returns to 1997-2005 Levels

Step 1

Apply the combined factor $c_j \, b_i \, a_j^S$ to each income item j on all returns <u>filed by any person represented on return i in 1987</u> in any year t (= 1988,…,1996). (These persons are members of the "cohort" portion of the panel.)

For returns filed by persons represented on "refreshment" returns (i.e., persons who first appear in the panel on a return filed[2] after 1987 by a non-dependent who was either a dependent in 1987 or immigrated to the United States after 1987), the super-cell S was identified in the first year the person filed a return. There is no factor b_i for refreshment returns, so the combined factor reduces to $c_j \, a_j^S$.

$$y_{ij}^{tE1} = c_j \, b_i \, a_j^S \, y_{ij}^t \qquad \text{for returns filed by cohort members of the panel}$$

$$y_{ij}^{tE1} = c_j \, a_j^S \, y_{ij}^t \qquad \text{for returns filed by refreshment members of the panel}$$

Steps 2-10

These Steps are analogous to Steps 6-14 of Section I, applied year-by-year. All of the formulas are the same, with the addition of a superscript t for the year. Step 10 completes the first extrapolation of the panel, to 1996-2005.

The second extrapolation, to the 2004-2013 period (the "04 budget period"), begins with a match of the 1987 records to the 2004 records from the first extrapolation. This requires the formation of super-cells and income and age quantiles within super-cells in the 2004 records,[3] reweighting 1987 records, and a micro-level record match of 1987 to

---

[2] No person represented in the refreshment segment of the panel entered the panel as a non-filer, but could become a non-filer in a subsequent year.

[3] The super-cell and income and age quantiles for 1987 records were formed in the first extrapolation. However, some different collapsing of super-cells or income or age quantiles might be required for consistency with the collapsing in the 2004 records.

2004 records. The second extrapolation then proceeds in steps that are nearly identical to the steps for the first extrapolation, so they are not described separately in this paper.

III. Source of Targets Uses in the Extrapolation

Targets for all variables were taken directly from, or derived from, the Administration's FY 04 Budget economic assumptions. Targets for income items reported on tax returns are determined by the Revenue Estimating Staff (RED) using historical relationships between tax return items and related income items included in the economic assumptions for the Budget. These targets are used in the second stage of the extrapolation of the ITM, so are referred to as "Stage 2" targets. These targets were obtained from RED and used directly in the panel model extrapolation, except for the transfer payments targets (social security and unemployment). Targets for all transfer payments, including social security and unemployment, covering all (filer and non-filer) recipients, were obtained from OMB. The following two tables show each targeted income item.

Items Reported on Tax Returns (Excluding Transfer Payments)

Income Item	Line on 1040	Variable Name
Wages	7	Wages and Salaries
Taxable interest	8a	Interest
Tax-exempt interest	8b	
Dividends	9	Div in AGI
Business (Schedule C) income	12	Sole Proprietor Income
Business (Schedule C) loss	12	
Capital gain in AGI	13	Pos CG, total
Taxable IRA and pension distributions	15b + 16b	Pension in AGI
Partnership (Schedule E) income	17 (part)	Partnership Net + (post-TRA)
Partnership (Schedule E) loss	17 (part)	Partnership Net − (post-TRA)
S Corp (Schedule E) income	17 (part)	Small Business + (post-TRA)
S Corp (Schedule E) loss	17 (part)	Small Business − (post-TRA)
Rental (Schedule E) income	17 (part)	Rent Net + (post-TRA)
Rental (Schedule E) loss	17 (part)	Rent Net − (post-TRA)
Farm (Schedule F) income	18 (part)	Farm Net +
Farm (Schedule F) loss	18 (part)	Farm Net -
All other items of gross income (except social security and unemployment)	10+11+ 13 (loss) +14+ 17 (part) +21	<No explicit Stage 2 target. MAGI is targeted, but it excludes some items of gross income and includes other items.>

Transfer Payments

Transfer Payment
Social Security & Railroad Retirement
Unemp Comp [Unemployment Compensation]
Workers Comp [Workers' Compensation Cash Benefits]
Veterans Pen/Dis [Veterans' Cash Pension and Disability Benefits]
SSI [Supplemental Security Income]
AFDC/TANF
Other Cash Assistance
Food Stamps

Several steps, and two spreadsheets, were used to compute the adjustment factors for certain itemized deductions, e_k and e_l (see Steps 11 and 12 of Section I). Most of the r factors (Step 11 of Section I) are "Stage I" per capita growth factors from the ITM extrapolation, or computed directly from these factors. For the 1996 and 1997, the Stage I per capita growth factors were taken from the 01MS (mid-session) extrapolation of the v15 ITM, and re-indexed to 1996.[4] The 04WB (winter budget) Stage I factors from RED were used for the 1998-2013 period, and re-indexed to 1996 for the first extrapolation and to 2004 for the second.

The remaining r factors require series for personal income, state and local income taxes, state and local property taxes, and consumer interest expense. For 1996 and 1997, these factors were computed from actuals from the NIPA and indexed to 1996. For the 1998-2013 period, these factors were computed from the Administration's "Black Box" forecasts for the 04WB and indexed to 1996 for the first extrapolation and to 2004 for the second.

The following table shows for each targeted itemized deduction's e factor the per capita growth factors used in the numerators (the r_k and r_l factors) and the specific source for the factor.

Factors for Targeted Itemized Deductions

Targeted Itemized Deduction	Numerator (r factor)	
	Stage I Factor	**Black Box Factor**
Investment Interest	--	consumer interest expense
Charitable	FCHAR	--

---

[4] The v15 ITM is based on the 1995 SOI, so Stage I growth factors for it are indexed to 1995 (i.e., 1995 = 1.0 for all factors).

Contributions		
S&L Income Taxes	--	S&L personal tax receipts
Mortgage Interest	--	50% personal income, 50% consumer interest expense
Medical	FMED	--
S&L Property Taxes	--	S&L property tax receipts

The denominators for the e factors, r_Y and r_{Y-G}, were calculated from the Stage 2 targets for MAGI, social security benefits, and capital gains.

APPENDIX D.3

Extrapolation: Shortcut Update

by

James R. Nunns

Short-Cut Update of the Panel Extrapolation to the WB 07 Budget Forecast

This paper provides a step-by-step algebraic description of the short-cut method for updating the current extrapolation of the panel, which is to the 04 budget period (2004-2013), to the WB forecast for the 07 budget period (2007-2016). This paper is a sequel to, Appendix D.2, "Algebraic Description of Panel Extrapolation," which should be read before this paper.[1] The update method described here is a short-cut because it simply applies adjustment factors to income and other items in the current extrapolation without creation of super-cells or any reweighting of returns.

The next section of the paper describes the short-cut method of updating the results from the current extrapolation for 2004-2013 to 2007-2016. Section II describes the separate income items (and groupings of items) that are to be used in the extrapolation and the extrapolation factors for detailed components of income and for non-income items.

I. Update the Results from the Current Extrapolation for 2004-2013 to 2007-2016 Levels

This update generally follows the last nine of the ten steps in Part II of the current extrapolation (see Appendix D.2, "Algebraic Description of Panel Extrapolation"). Return-level (unweighted) variables are denoted with lower-case letters, y and x, and weighted and aggregate variables by upper case letters, Y and X. Superscripts generally give the Budget forecast (04 or 07) first, followed by the year, t, where $t = 2004,\ldots,2013$ in Steps 1-3, and $2007,\ldots,2016$ in Steps 4-9. Note that for the 04 Budget extrapolation, each year is lagged three years from the 07 Budget extrapolation, although they are the same year for each return; for example, a (original 1987) return that represents 2004 in the current (04 Budget) extrapolation (i.e., superscript 0404) will represent a 2007 return in the updated (WB 07 Budget) extrapolation (i.e., superscript 0707).

Step 1

Compute for all returns (including dependents' and "refreshment" returns) the sum of each income item j:

$$Y_j^{04t} = \sum_i Y_{ij}^{04t}$$

where Y_{ij}^{04t} is the weighted amount of

$$y_{ij}^{04t}$$

---

[1] In Appendix D.2, "Algebraic Description of Panel Extrapolation," the extrapolation to the 2004-2013 period is referred to as the "second" extrapolation, to distinguish it from the beginning extrapolation (to the 1996-2005 period), but is referred to in this paper simply as the "current" extrapolation.

Note that for income items included in gross income (except social security and UI benefits), the sum is computed only for filers (including dependent filers) since the targets for these items are only for filers.

Step 2

Compute the ratio c_j^t for each income item j where:

$$c_j^t = Y_j^{07T(t+3)} / Y_j^{04t}$$

where $Y_j^{07T(t+3)}$ is the WB 07 Budget target for income source j in year $t+3$

Note that for income items included in gross income (except social security and UI benefits), the ratio is computed only for filers (including dependent filers) since the targets for these items are only for filers.

Step 3

Apply c_j^t to income item j on all returns (filer, including dependent, and non-filer) to give the updated (WB 07 Budget) extrapolation for income items.

$$y_{ij}^{07(t+3)} = c_j^t \, y_{ij}^{04t}$$

Steps 4 and 5 use the income as adjusted in the preceding steps to develop adjustment factors, and Step 6 applies these factors or the c_j^t ratios to components of 1040 income items (e.g., the detailed components from Schedules C, D, E, F) and to exogenous non-income items.

Step 4

Compute the total income, and total income without capital gains, from Step 3 on each return i in each year t:

$$y_i^{07t} = \sum_j y_{ij}^{07t}$$

and

$$(y_i^{07t} - y_{ig}^{07t})$$

where y_{ig}^{07t} is capital gains on return i

Step 5

Compute for each year t the ratio of total income, with and without capital gains, from Step 4 to the corresponding amounts from the current (04 Budget) extrapolation for each return i:

$$d_i^{tW} = y_i^{07t} / y_i^{04(t-3)}$$

and

$$d_i^{tWO} = (y_i^{07t} - y_{ig}^{07t})/(y_i^{04(t-3)} - y_{ig}^{04(t-3)})$$

Step 6

Apply d_i^{tW} to state and local income taxes, investment interest expense, and charitable contributions (items denoted with the subscript k in the following steps) on all returns i in each year t (that have itemized deductions);

Apply d_i^{tWO} to medical expenses, state and local property and other (non-income) taxes, home mortgage interest expense, casualty and theft losses, and miscellaneous itemized deductions (those denoted with the subscript l in the following steps) on all returns i in each year t (that have itemized deductions).

Apply d_i^{tW}, d_i^{tWO}, or the appropriate c_j^t ratio to the components of income and the remaining exogenous non-income items (those denoted with the subscript m) on all returns i in each year t. See Section II for a description of which factor applies to each of these items.

Application of these factors updates the extrapolation of components of income and exogenous non-income items (except itemized deductions; see Steps 7-9) to the WB 07 Budget forecast.

$$x_{ik}^{07t} = d_i^{tW} x_{ik}^{04(t-3)}$$ where x_{ik}^{*t} is the amount of itemized deduction k on return i in year t

$$x_{il}^{07t} = d_i^{tWO} x_{il}^{04(t-3)}$$ where x_{il}^{*t} is the amount of itemized deduction l on return i in year t

and

$$x_{im}^{07t} = c_j^t x_{im}^{04(t-3)}$$ where x_{im}^{*t} is the amount of income component or non-income item m on return i in year t

or

$$d_i^{tW} x_{im}^{04(t-3)}$$

or

$$d_i^{tWO} \; x_{im}^{04(t-3)}$$

Steps 7-9 adjust the amounts of itemized deductions on all returns from Step 6 for differential growth rates forecasted for these deductions relative to total income or total income without capital gains. Note that Steps 7 and 8 are computed in the spreadsheet: Panel Model_Extrapolation to WB FY07 budget period.xls. Also, there is no differential growth rate for casualty and theft and miscellaneous itemized deductions, so the ratios for them (Step 8) are 1.0 in all years (i.e., the ratios need not be applied).

Step 7

Compute from the WB 07 Budget forecast the per capita growth rates of total income and total income without capital gains and the per capita growth rates for itemized deductions.

$$r_Y^t = (Y^t / N^t)/(Y^{t-1}/N^{t-1})$$

$$r_{Y-G}^t = ((Y^t - Y_g^t)/N^t)/((Y^{t-1} - Y_g^{t-1})/N^{t-1})$$

r_k^t = the per capita growth rate computed from Budget forecast variables for itemized deduction k (see Section II of the paper)

r_l^t = the per capita growth rate computed from Budget forecast variables for itemized deduction l (see Section II of the paper)

Step 8

Compute the ratio e_k^t or e_l^t for each targeted itemized deduction k or l:

$$e_k^t = r_k^t / r_Y^t$$
$$e_l^t = r_l^t / r_{Y-G}^t$$

Step 9

Apply e_k^t (e_l^t) to itemized deductions k (l), as adjusted in Step 6 of all returns i in each year t. This completes the update of the extrapolation for these itemized deductions.

$$x_{ik}^{07t} = e_k^t \; x_{ik}^{07t}$$

$$x_{il}^{07t} = e_l^t \; x_{il}^{07t}$$

II. Income Forecasts and Extrapolation Factors

Table 1 shows sources for the $Y_j^{07T(t+3)}$ variables in Step 2, above, to compute the c_j^t factors applied to the corresponding income items in Step 3, and the e_k^t and e_l^t factors for Step 9 (Steps 7 and 8 are performed in a spreadsheet).

Table 2 indicates which c_j^t factor or whether d_i^{tW} or d_i^{tWO} applies to each component of income or each exogenous non-income item in Step 6.

Table 1. Sources of Targets for Income Items

	Line on (2001) 1040 (Schedule E)	SOI Variable (TY2001)	ITM (v17) Variable	ITM WB 07 Budget Extrapolation Variable		Panel Model Variable[1]
				Stage 2 Target	Stage 1 Factor	
Income Items with Targets for Filers Only						
Wages	7	E00200	was	Wages and Salaries	FWAGE	
Taxable interest	8a	E00300	intst	Interest	FINTER	
Tax-exempt interest	8b	E00400	texint			
Dividends	9	E00600	dbe	Div in AGI	FDIV	
S&L income tax refunds	10	E00700	sitr			
Alimony received	11	E00800			FWAGE	alimony
Business (Schedule C) income or loss	12	E00900	bil	Sole Proprietor Income FSLTAX	FNFBUSI	
Capital gain in AGI	13 (pos.)	E01000 +	<calculator variables>	Pos CG, total	FLCAPGL	
Capital loss in AGI	13 (neg.)	E01100 –				
Other gains or losses	14	E01200	suppgl		FLCAPGL	
Taxable IRA distributions	15b	E01400	tirad	Taxable IRA Distributions	FTIRAD	
Taxable pension distributions	16b	E01700	ptpen	Pension in AGI	FPENS	ptpexc
Rental income	17 (part of 26) (pos.)	E27310 – E25800 –	rent	Rent Net +	FRENTG	
Rental loss	17 (part of 26) (neg.)	E27200		Rent Net -	FRENTL	
Royalty income or loss	17 (part of 26)	E25800	royal		FRENTG	

	Line on (2001) 1040 (Schedule E)	SOI Variable (TY2001)	ITM (v17) Variable	ITM WB 07 Budget Extrapolation Variable		Panel Model Variable[1]
				Stage 2 Target	Stage 1 Factor	
Partnership income	17 (part of 32) (pos.)	-E25920 +E25940 +E25980	part	Partnership Net +	FPRTNRG	
Partnership loss	17 (part of 32) (neg.)	-E25960 -E26110		Partnership Net -	FPRTNRL	
S Corp. income	17 (part of 32) (pos.)	-E26100 -E26160	sbc	Small Business +	FSCORPG	
S Corp. loss	17 (part of 32) (neg.)	+E26170 -E26180 +E26190		Small Business -	FSCORPL	
Estate and trust income or loss	17 (37)	E26500	estu		FGNP	
Farm rental income or loss	17 (40)	E27200	frnt		FFBUSI	
Farm income	18 (pos.)	E02100	fil	Farm Net +	FFBUSI	
Farm loss	18 (neg.)			Farm Net -		
Other income — NOLs		E02540	nols			
Other income — Gambling	21	E02800	gamble		FGNP	N/A
Other income — Other		E02600	othinc			
Other income — Sec. 911 income exclusion		E02700	forexc		FWAGE < calculator caps>	
Income Items with Targets for All Units (Filers and Non-Filers)						
Social security & RRB benefits		ssine				
Unemployment compensation			ucagix			
Workers compensation						wkcmp

Line on (2001) 1040 (Schedule E)	SOI Variable (TY2001)	ITM (v17) Variable	ITM WB 07 Budget Extrapolation Variable		Panel Model Variable[1]
			Stage 2 Target	Stage 1 Factor	
Veterans cash pension & disability benefits					vet
SSI					ssi
AFDC/TANF					afdc
State general assistance					Welf
State energy assistance					heat
Other State cash assist.					unktr
Food stamps					food

[1] The panel model variable is the same as the ITM variable unless otherwise noted. N/A indicates the variable is not on the panel model.

D.3 - 8

Table 2. Sources of Targets for Income Detail Items and Non-Income Items

Item	Line on 2001 Schedule or Form	SOI Variable (TY 2001)	ITM (v17) Variable	ITM WB 07 Budget Stage 1 Factor	Panel Model Variable[1]	Panel Model d_i^t or c_j^t Factor
Additional 1040 Income Items						
Total IRA distributions	15a	E01300	girad	FTIRAD		c_j^t (tirad)
Total pension distributions	16a	E01800	ptpenex	FPENS	ptpen	c_j^t (ptpexc)
		<computed>	fellow	FGNP		c_j^t (othinc)
		<computed>	resid	<computed post-extrap>		<computed post-extrap>
		<computed>	agimod			
W-2 Items						
			o401k p	FWAGE	N/A	c_j^t (was)
			o401k s		N/A	
			hiexcl p		N/A	N/A
			hiexcl s		N/A	
			depcare p	FCPI	N/A	
			depcare s		N/A	
Schedule B (Interest and Ordinary Dividends) Detail						
Savings bond interest	3	E21100	savbond	FINTER		c_j^t (intst)
Schedule C (Sole Proprietor) Detail						
		<2001 levels computed pre-extrap.>	pschc	FNBUSI		c_j^t (bil)
			alt pschc			
		<computed>				
	31 (all Cs)	E90440	sch c		N/A	N/A

D.3 - 9

aschcg

Schedule D (Capital Gains) Detail

Item	Line on 2001 Schedule or Form	SOI Variable (TY 2001)	ITM (v17) Variable	ITM WB 07 Budget Stage 1 Factor	Panel Model Variable[1]	Panel Model d_i^t or c_j^t Factor
	31 (1ˢᵗ C)	E91440	schc 1		N/A	
	31 (2ⁿᵈ C)	E92440	schc 2		N/A	
	31 (3ʳᵈ C)	E93440	schc 3		N/A	
			smiscg			
			smiscl			
			spartg			
			spartl			
	E21610	E21800	p69stc			
	E21615		stg			
	E21700		stl	FSCAPGL		c_j^t (cg in AGI)
	E21750		sndedl			
<All short-term items>	5	E21775	nspartgl			
	E21850	<legacy>	cystg			
	E21900	<legacy>	cystl			
	E22260	<legacy>	N/A			
			lmiscg			
			lmiscl			
			lpartg			
			lpartl			
	13 E22310	E22370	lcgd			
<All long-term items>	14 E22315	E22390	p69ltc	FLCAPGL	srescg	c_j^t (cg in AGI)
	E22350		ltg			c_j^t (cg in AGI)
	E22360		ltl			
			lndedl			
	17	E23660	undyco			
	E22400					
	E22500					
	E23300					

D.3 - 10

Item	Line on 2001 Schedule or Form	SOI Variable (TY 2001)	ITM (v17) Variable	ITM WB 07 Budget Stage 1 Factor	Panel Model Variable[1]	Panel Model d_i^t or c_j^t Factor
		<legacy>	cyltg			
		<legacy>	cyltl			
		<computed>	pcapl			
	2	E21600	nssocagl		N/A	N/A
	4	E21620	nsmiscgl		N/A	c_j^t (cg in AGI)
	11(g)	E22325	lmisc28		N/A	
	12(g)	E22367	lpart28		N/A	N/A
	13(g)	E22375	lcgd28		N/A	
	14(g)	E22395	p69ltc28		N/A	
	9(f)	E22300	nlsocagl			
	11(f)	E22320	nlmiscgl			c_j^t (cg in AGI)
	12(f)	E22365	nlpartgl			
			lsoca28		N/A	
	32	E24590	gain10		N/A	N/A
	36	E24600	gain20		N/A	
			gain25		N/A	
	E22305		gain28		N/A	
			N/A		lrescg	
			N/A		linstlg	
	E24610		N/A		llikekg	c_j^t (cg in AGI)
	E24550		N/A		llikekl	
			N/A		l4797	
Collectibles at 28%	15(g)	E22550	cg28pct	<no growth>	N/A	N/A

Schedule E Detail – Rents

		<2001 levels	rentg	FRENTG (if rent +)		c_j^t (rent)
		computed	rentl			

Item	Line on 2001 Schedule or Form	SOI Variable (TY 2001)	ITM (v17) Variable	ITM WB 07 Budget Stage 1 Factor	Panel Model Variable[1]	Panel Model d_i^t or c_j^t Factor
		pre-extrap.>	rent			
	3 (total)	E25350	trent	FRENTL (if rent -)		
		E25830	edisrent			

Schedule E Detail – Royalties

Item	Line on 2001 Schedule or Form	SOI Variable (TY 2001)	ITM (v17) Variable	ITM WB 07 Budget Stage 1 Factor	Panel Model Variable[1]	Panel Model d_i^t or c_j^t Factor
		E25800	royal (= troyal + rentdepr)	FRENTG (if royal +) FRENTL (if royal -)		c_j^t (royal)

Schedule E Detail – Partnership

Item	Line on 2001 Schedule or Form	SOI Variable (TY 2001)	ITM (v17) Variable	ITM WB 07 Budget Stage 1 Factor	Panel Model Variable[1]	Panel Model d_i^t or c_j^t Factor
23 <All items>	apart	<2001 levels computed	part	FPRTNRG (if part +)		c_j^t (part)
	bpart	pre-extrap.>	alt ppart			
		<computed>				
	27(k)	E25980	apartg			
	27(i)	-E25960	apartl	FPRTNRL (if part -)		
	27(j)	-E26110	ppartg			
	27(h)	E25940	ppartl			
	27(g)	-E25920				

Schedule E Detail – S Corporations

Item	Line on 2001 Schedule or Form	SOI Variable (TY 2001)	ITM (v17) Variable	ITM WB 07 Budget Stage 1 Factor	Panel Model Variable[1]	Panel Model d_i^t or c_j^t Factor
22 <All items>	apart	<2001 levels computed	sbc	FSCORPG (if sbc +)		c_j^t (sbc)
	bpart	pre-extrap.>	asbcg			
	27(i)	E26190	asbcl	FSCORPL (if sbc -)		
	27(j)	-E26180	psbcg			
	27(h)	-E26100	psbcl			
	27(g)	E26170				
		-E26160				

Schedule E Detail – Estate and Trust

asbc
psbc

Item	Line on 2001 Schedule or Form	SOI Variable (TY 2001)	ITM (v17) Variable	ITM WB 07 Budget Stage 1 Factor	Panel Model Variable[1]	Panel Model d_i^t or c_j^t Factor
<All items>		<2001 levels computed pre-extrap.>				c_j^t (estu)
	33a(f)	E26380	estu / aestug	FGNP		
	33b(e)	-E26360	aestu / aestul			
	33a(d)	E26340	psetug			
	33b(c)	-E26320	pestul			

Schedule E Detail – Farm Rental Income

Item	Line on 2001 Schedule or Form	SOI Variable (TY 2001)	ITM (v17) Variable	ITM WB 07 Budget Stage 1 Factor	Panel Model Variable[1]	Panel Model d_i^t or c_j^t Factor
<All items>		<2001 levels computed pre-extrap.>	pfrntg	FFBUSI		c_j^t (frnt)
	39	E27200	frnt			

Schedule E Detail – Total

Item	Line on 2001 Schedule or Form	SOI Variable (TY 2001)	ITM (v17) Variable	ITM WB 07 Budget Stage 1 Factor	Panel Model Variable[1]	Panel Model d_i^t or c_j^t Factor
	psetu	<computed>	sch e	<computed post-extrap>	sche	<computed post-extrap>

Form 8582 (Passive Losses) Detail

Item	Line on 2001 Schedule or Form	SOI Variable (TY 2001)	ITM (v17) Variable	ITM WB 07 Budget Stage 1 Factor	Panel Model Variable[1]	Panel Model d_i^t or c_j^t Factor
<Rental items +>	1a	E65300	z1a	FRENTG		c_j^t (rent)
	1d	E65600	z1d			
<Rental items ->	1b	E65400	z1b	FRENTL		c_j^t (rent)
<Partnership items +>	2a	E66000	z2a	FPRTNRG		c_j^t (part)
	2d	E66300	z2d			
<Partnership items ->	2b	E66100	z2b	FPRTNRL		c_j^t (part)
		<computed>	agiuks	FGNP		c_j^t (part)
			allow01			
			plossnd	FCPI		c_j^t (part)
			ndirap			
			ndiras			

E68000
E90640
E68500
E68505

Schedule F (Farm Proprietor) Detail

Item	Line on 2001 Schedule or Form	SOI Variable (TY 2001)	ITM (v17) Variable	ITM WB 07 Budget Stage 1 Factor	Panel Model Variable[1]	Panel Model d_i^t or c_j^t Factor
<All items>		<2001 levels computed pre-extrap.>	afarmg afarml pfarmg pfarml afarm	FFBUSI		c_j^t (fil)
		<computed>	pfarm alt pfarm			
	36 (all Fs)	E95640	farm		N/A	N/A
	36 (1st F)	E96640	farm_1		N/A	
	36 (2nd F)	E97640	farm_2		N/A	
			pfarmnd		N/A	

Form 2555 (Foreign Earned Income Exclusion) Detail

Form 1040 -- Adjustments to Income ("Above the Line Deductions")

Item	Line on 2001 Schedule or Form	SOI Variable (TY 2001)	ITM (v17) Variable	ITM WB 07 Budget Stage 1 Factor	Panel Model Variable[1]	Panel Model d_i^t or c_j^t Factor
	23 E95660	E03150	adjira		adjira_p adjira_s	<no growth>
IRA contributions			zadjira	<no growth>	N/A	
Student loan interest	24	E03210	ed_ded	FCPI	N/A	N/A
Moving expenses	26	E03280	exmove	FWAGE		c_j^t (was)
Archer MSA	25	E03600		FMED	N/A	N/A
Self-employed health	28	E03270	healse			c_j^t (bil)
Keogh contributions	29	E03300	keogh	FG401		c_j^t (was)
Alimony paid	31a	E03500		FCPI	alimpd	d_i^{two}
					ebe_aj	d_i^{two}

Item	Line on 2001 Schedule or Form	SOI Variable (TY 2001)	ITM (v17) Variable	ITM WB 07 Budget Stage 1 Factor	Panel Model Variable[1]	Panel Model d_i^t or c_j^t Factor
Interest penalty	30	E03400			pen int	c_j^t (intst)
SECA deduction (50%)	27	E03260			secaded (computed)	<computed post-extrap>
Other adjustments		E03900				
Foreign housing exclusion	32 (margin entry)	E04000	forhe	FGNP		c_j^t (othinc)
		<computed>	adjust	<computed post-extrap>		<computed post-extrap>

Schedule A (Itemized Deductions)

Item	Line on 2001 Schedule or Form	SOI Variable (TY 2001)	ITM (v17) Variable	ITM WB 07 Budget Stage 1 Factor	Panel Model Variable[1]	Panel Model d_i^t or c_j^t Factor
Medical and dental	1	E17500	ttmed	FMED		d_i^{two}
State and local taxes	9	E18300	ttsltx			<computed post-extrap>
	5	E18400	slitx	FSLTAX		d_i^{tw}
	6	E18500	retx			d_i^{two}
	7	E18800	pptx			d_i^{two}
	8	E18900	otsltx			d_i^{two}
Home mortgage interest	10 + 11	E19300	hmie	FHOMEI		d_i^{two}
	12	E19530	points			
Investment interest	13 (part)	E19575	oth_ie	FINTEXP	cie	d_i^{tw}
					cie ded	
Charitable contributions	18	E19700	ttcon	FCHARG		d_i^{tw}
	15	E19800	tcash			
Casualty and theft	19	<computed>	ttcasu	FCPI		d_i^{two}

Item	Line on 2001 Schedule or Form	SOI Variable (TY 2001)	ITM (v17) Variable	ITM WB 07 Budget Stage 1 Factor	Panel Model Variable[1]	Panel Model d_i^t or c_j^t Factor
Miscellaneous deductions, 2% floor	23	E20400	t2misc [pre-limitation]	FCPI	dedmis [computed allowable]	d_i^{two}
					ebe	
Gambling losses	27 (part)	E20900	fdgamb	FCPI		d_i^{two}
Other miscellaneous	27 (part)	E21000	fdmisc	FCPI	fdothd	d_i^{two}
Form 4952 (Investment Interest Expense Deduction)						
	3	E58950	gr tiie	FINTEXP		d_i^{tw}
		<computed>	tiie oth			
	5	E59100	yinv exp	FGNP		d_i^{tw}
		<computed>	yinv uks			
			tcga inv	FLCAPGL		c_j^t (cg in AGI)
			supp inv			
	E58980		nstgl_inv	SLCAPGL		c_j^t (cg in AGI)
	<legacy>	<legacy>	cg elct			
	<computed>	<computed>	pct elct	<no growth>		<no growth>
Special Tax Amounts						
Tax from Form 8615	40 E58990	E74160	txkidx	<computed post-extrap>		<computed post-extrap>
Tax from Form 8814 or 4972	40	E05700	spcta_	FTAXGR	spctax	d_i^{tw}
Form 8615 (Kiddie tax)						
	2	E72900	dedkid	FGNP		d_i^{two}
		<computed>	tih nocg		N/A	N/A

Item	Line on 2001 Schedule or Form	SOI Variable (TY 2001)	ITM (v17) Variable	ITM WB 07 Budget Stage 1 Factor	Panel Model Variable[1]	Panel Model d_i^t or c_j^t Factor
		<computed>	oui_nocg		N/A	
		E73650		FLCAPGL		c_j^t (cg in AGI)
		<SOI no longer collects>	inlcgh			
		<computed>	inlcgo		N/A	N/A
		<computed>	unuse_cg		N/A	N/A
		<computed>	dmfsh	<no growth>		<no growth>
		<computed>	unk_kidi	FDIV		c_j^t (dbe)
		<computed>	stxkid	FSLTAX		d_i^{tw}
		E74160	txwoui	<computed post-extrap>		<computed post-extrap>
		E82100	amtcr_cf	FTAXGR		d_i^{tw}
	6	E73200	tikidh	<computed post-extrap>		<computed post-extrap>
	7	E73300	ouikid			
Form 8814 (Parents' Elective Kiddie Tax)						
	1a (1st 8814)	E83060		FINTER		c_j^t (intst)
	1a (2nd 8814)	E83460				
	1a (3rd 8814)	E83860		FDIV		c_j^t (dbe)
	6 (4+ 8814)	E84210	pe_agi4			
	E83140		tcgkid1		N/A	
	E83540		tcgkid2	FLCAPGL	N/A	N/A
	E83940		tcgkid3		N/A	
	3 (total)	E84185	pe_lcgd		N/A	
	E83185					
	E83585					
	E83985					

Item	Line on 2001 Schedule or Form	SOI Variable (TY 2001)	ITM (v17) Variable	ITM WB 07 Budget Stage 1 Factor	Panel Model Variable[1]	Panel Model d_i^t or c_j^t Factor
		E83160	dikid1			
			dikid2			
		<computed>	dikid3	<computed post-extrap>		<computed post-extrap>
			dikidt			
			pe_inagi			
	9 (4+ E84560	E84220	pe_tax4			
	E83960					

Form 6251 (AMT)

Item	Line on 2001 Schedule or Form	SOI Variable (TY 2001)	ITM (v17) Variable	ITM WB 07 Budget Stage 1 Factor	Panel Model Variable[1]	Panel Model d_i^t or c_j^t Factor
	17	E60100	amtnol	FGNP		d_i^{tw}
	E84180		amtnol alt			
	25	E62900	amtftc			
		<computed>	ucamti	<set to zero>		<set to zero>
	E62000	<legacy>	entpref	FPREF		d_i^{tw}
		<computed>	prefaj			
		<computed>	timepref		N/A	N/A
		<computed>	adjvui			
		<computed>	pref_impt			d_i^{tw}
		<computed>	amtuexm			
		<computed>	capgains_diff	FLCAPGL	N/A	N/A
					N/A	
					N/A	

Form 1116 (Foreign Tax Credit)

Item	Line on 2001 Schedule or Form	SOI Variable (TY 2001)	ITM (v17) Variable	ITM WB 07 Budget Stage 1 Factor	Panel Model Variable[1]	Panel Model d_i^t or c_j^t Factor
		<computed>	tftccr	FGNP		d_i^{tw}

Form 2441 (CDCTC)

Item	Line on 2001 Schedule or Form	SOI Variable (TY 2001)	ITM (v17) Variable	ITM WB 07 Budget Stage 1 Factor	Panel Model Variable[1]	Panel Model d_i^t or c_j^t Factor
	1d (total)	E32700	ccecyr	FCPI		c_j^t (was)
	18	E32840	exclcc			
	6	E33300	cccpyr			
	10	E33420	emplycc			

d_line27_diff
cg25pct_diff

Item	Line on 2001 Schedule or Form	SOI Variable (TY 2001)	ITM (v17) Variable	ITM WB 07 Budget Stage 1 Factor	Panel Model Variable[1]	Panel Model d_i^t or c_j^t Factor
	11	E33450	cclost			
	13	E33460	empcce			
	19	E33480	taxcce			
		<computed>	cce_nq			
	15	E32880	ccei_p	FWAGE		c_j^t (was)
	16	E32890	cdei_s			
		F2441	ccqi	<no growth>		<no growth>
Schedule R (Elderly Credit)						
			tdiinc			d_i^{tW}
	11	E28200	eldtxi	FCPI		
	13c	E28400	eldnti			
Form 8863 (Hope and Lifetime Learning Credits)						
	E28100		tuition_hope	FCPI	N/A [Tuition expenses imputed post-extrap from different variables.]	
		<imputed>	tuition_life			
		<computed>	tuition_hope	<computed post-extrap>		
Form 8839 (Adoption Credit)						
			adopt_exp_1	FCPI	N/A	N/A
			adopt_exp_2			
From 3800 (General Business Credit)	tuition_hope| tuition_hope| E53220	cyitc	FBUSCR		d_i^{two}
	1b	E86100 E53240	jobs			
	1d	E86110 E53260	fuel			
	1e	E53280	raecr			

D.3 - 19

Item	Line on 2001 Schedule or Form	SOI Variable (TY 2001)	ITM (v17) Variable	ITM WB 07 Budget Stage 1 Factor	Panel Model Variable[1]	Panel Model d_i^t or c_j^t Factor
	1f	E53300	lihcr			
	1g	E53305	enoil			
	1h	E53310	diacr			
	1i	E53315	elecpr			
	1j	E53316	indemp		N/A	N/A
	1k	E53317	sstips		N/A	
	1m	E53312	? [New markets]		N/A	
	1n	E53319	ccdccr			d_i^t
	1p	E53313	cycelpcr			
	3	E53340	ptter			
	5	E53380	pdiscr			
	6	E53400	gbcyo			
	1c	E53250	to worker		N/A	N/A
	1o	E53314	tr alaska		N/A	
	1l	E53318	orphan dr		N/A	
	18c	E53487	susp re		N/A	d_i^{two}
					esopcr	
			Form 8396 (Mortgage Interest Credit)			
	3	E64000	cytmicr			d_i^{two}
	6	E64060	tmc cyo1	FGNP		
	5	E64040	tmc cyo2			
	4	E64020	tmc cyo3			
			Form 8844 (Empowerment Zone Credit)			
		E75000	tezecr	FGNP	N/A	N/A
			Other Credits			
		E07500	ezecr	FBUSCR		
		E07900	fuels nc			d_i^{two}
		E08000	othcr			

Item	Line on 2001 Schedule or Form	SOI Variable (TY 2001)	ITM (v17) Variable	ITM WB 07 Budget Stage 1 Factor	Panel Model Variable[1]	Panel Model d_i^t or c_j^t Factor
		E07950	dc homecr	FGNP	N/A	N/A
		<computed>	unlimcr			d_i^{two}
Schedule SE (Self Employment (SECA) Tax)						
	1 (total)	E29000	sefarm			
	1 (p)	E29020	sefarmp			
	1 (s)	E29050	sefarms	FFBUSI		c_j^t (fil)
	15 (total)	E31150	optfarm			
	15 (p)	E31170	optfarmp			
	15 (s)	E31200	optfarms			
	2 (total)	E29070	Senonf			
	2 (p)	E29100	senonfp	FNFBUSI <u>or</u> 1.0		c_j^t (bil) <u>or</u> 1.0
	2 (s)	E29120	senonfs			
	17 (total)	E31220	optnonf			
	17 (p)	E31250	optnonfp	<factor computed>		<factor computed>
	17 (s)	E31300	optnonfs			
	5a (total)	E30100	chwas			
	5a (p)	E30200	chwasp			
	5a (s)	E30300	chwass	FWAGE		c_j^t (was)
	8c (p)	E29400	wasp oas			
	8c (s)	E29450	wass oas			
		<computed>	seernp			
		<computed>	seerns	<computed post-extrap>		<computed post-extrap>
		<computed>	seerm			
Other Taxes						
	56	E10000	adveic	FWAGE		c_j^t (was)
	57	E10050	schh tx		N/A	N/A
Payments						

Item	Line on 2001 Schedule or Form	SOI Variable (TY 2001)	ITM (v17) Variable	ITM WB 07 Budget Stage 1 Factor	Panel Model Variable[1]	Panel Model d_i^t or c_j^t Factor
	59	E10700	with	FWAGE		c_j^t (was)
	60	E10900	esttax	FTAXGR		d_i^{tW}
EITC						
		E59520	utearn	FWAGE		c_j^t (was)
		<computed>	ueicei	FCPI		d_i^{tW}
		E59680	eicoff	N/A	N/A	N/A
		E59720	eicref	<no growth>	N/A	
Social Security Taxes						
		E30700	seta p			
		E30800	seta s			
		E30600	seta	<computed post-extrap>	[All calculated, but different names]	<computed post-extrap>
		<computed>	secat			
61b		E82910-E11200	ss employee			

[1] The panel model variable is the same as the ITM variable unless otherwise noted.

N/A indicates the variable is not on the model.

APPENDIX D.4

Extrapolation: Estate Tax Data

by

Deena Ackerman

Estate Tax Data

This appendix describes the annual extrapolation of the estate tax model to the current budget period. Every year we target the official Winter Budget forecast of estate and gift tax liabilities (net of refunds) when computing estate tax liability under current law. Targets for Pre-EGTRRA and TRA86 liabilities are computed relative to the Winter Budget forecast.

I. Estate and Gift Tax Liability Estimates

Every year, the Revenue Estimating Division of the Office of Tax Analysis forecasts estate and gift tax receipts for that year's budget window. To construct these forecasts, the revenue estimator uses the most recent SOI estate tax file (currently 2005) augmented with SOI estate tax data from 2001. The recent data is augmented with older data because the relatively high exemption level under current law means that the most recent data includes no information on smaller estates. (In 2005 the exclusion level was $1.5 million. In contrast, in 2001 the exemption was only $675 thousand.) Information on the smaller estates is necessary for forecasting liabilities in the later years of the budget period, (and in the panel, for estimating liabilities under pre-EGTRRA and TRA86 law). Although these estates contribute only a small share of total estate tax revenue, there are a relatively large number of such estates.

II. Creating a Set of Targets

The panel staff is also supplied with a set of unadjusted estate tax liabilities under current law (EGTRRA), and under TRA86 and TRA87 law (Pre-EGTRRA). The unadjusted liability estimates used in this model differ slightly from the official Revenue Estimating liability estimates because the official estimates involve additional off-model adjustments to account for discrepancies in when the estate taxes are paid. Therefore, we create a set of factors (one for each year in the budget window) that adjust the first round estimates for the off-model adjustments.

The unadjusted estate tax liability estimates for TRA86 and for TRA87 are multiplied by these factors to create the relevant adjusted estate tax liability estimates. Gift taxes estimates are calculated as a fixed percentage of the adjusted estate tax liabilities under pre-EGTRRA and TRA86 law. These shares are 14 and 15 percent respectively.

III. Estimating Extrapolated Estate Tax Liabilities On the Panel Model.

Once all six targets (estate and gift taxes, each under the three laws) for each year have been specified, the next step is to estimate extrapolated estate tax liabilities on the panel model. For each panel member for whom an estate tax return was filed, estate tax liability is estimated under current law, pre-EGTRRA law and TRA86 law in the following way.

For each panel member who died during the period, the gross value of their estate is inflated from the year of death to their extrapolated year in the budget window. Thus, with a budget period of 2008-2017, the extrapolated year of death would be 2011 for a panel member who died in 1990 (the 4th year of the panel). The gross value of the estate is inflated by a factor that captures macroeconomic and demographic growth changes over the relevant period.

Then, by applying a simplified estate tax model calculator to the gross estate, we compute an estimate of the estate tax owed under each of the three tax regimes.

In each case, estimates are provided as if the panel members "died" in their extrapolated year of death, and again when the date of death is extrapolated to the first year in the budget period. By extrapolating all deaths to the first year in the budget period, we are able to mitigate some of the effects of the relatively small number of deaths in any given year.

IV. Rescaling the Panel Estimates to Hit the Targets

As above, estimated liability will differ from the official estimates due to off-model calculations. However, estimated liability will also differ from the targets due to differences between the characteristics of the SOI sample and the panel sample. Using the six targets specified above (the current law liability estimates for estate and gift, along with the scaled estimates under pre-EGTRRA law and TRA86 law), we create an additional set of factors which force the panel estimates to be identical in aggregate to the adjusted SOI estimates for each law in each year. Current law gift tax liabilities are computed so that the ratio between targeted estate tax liability and targeted gift tax liability is maintained.

APPENDIX E

Equivalence Scales

by

Julie-Anne Cronin

Equivalence Scales

I. Overview

This paper describes the equivalence scale that Treasury's Office of Tax Analysis (OTA) uses in its multi-year distributional analyses, and shows how that scale may affect the distribution of income and tax burdens.

In its single-year tables, OTA does not use an equivalence scale to adjust income for family size. Families are ranked based only on the family's income; for example, a family of four with $40,000 of income is ranked as having the same ability to pay as a family of one with $40,000. Implicitly, this treats families as if they enjoy perfect returns to scale; additional family members do not lower the well-being of the family.

In contrast, the multi-year period of OTA's new distributional analyses necessitates an explicit adjustment for family size. In these multi-year analyses, the income and tax burdens of base-year families are measured over the ten-year budget period. Because family composition changes over the budget period, a base-year family's income and tax burden cannot be measured in each year of the budget period. Instead, the income and tax burdens for each individual who existed in the base year are measured in each year. The equivalence scale used for this measure determines how a family's income is translated into the income of each individual in the family in each year. If the equivalence scale assumes perfect returns to scale, each individual in a given family in a given year would be assigned the family's income for that year. At the other extreme, if the equivalence scale assumes no returns to scale then the family's income in each year would be divided by the number of individuals in the family. OTA's equivalence scale falls between these two extremes.

II. Assumptions

The following assumptions hold under both single-year and multi-year analyses:

- Equal welfare of family members: Families are assumed to act as an economic unit, sharing both resources and costs. This is implicit in OTA's single-year income measure, and also applies to the multi-year, equivalence scale-adjusted measure. The sources of income do not matter in assigning income to family members. For example, if all family income is derived from the earning of one member, that member is not assigned a different level of welfare than the non-working members. Likewise, tax burdens are assumed to be shared equally among family members.

- Income as a proxy for welfare: Income is used as a proxy for welfare. An important difference between income and welfare measures is that an income measure omits the value of leisure time. If two otherwise identical families (or individuals) have the same wage income but have different levels of work effort, they will have the same rank under an income measure even though their welfare is obviously not equivalent.

Another important difference is that welfare measures control for differences in prices faced by consumers. If two otherwise identical families have the same income but one lives in a high cost-of-living area, the two families would have the same rank under an income measure even though the purchasing power of the family living in the high cost of living area is considerably lower. Finally, forward-looking welfare measures consider the degree of uncertainty surrounding earnings and consumption choices; income measures do not.

OTA's choice of income as a proxy for welfare is based on several considerations. Although income may not be a good proxy for welfare in some instances, income is measured with a relatively high degree of precision whereas the value of leisure, the prices faced by different families, and uncertainty of income and consumption streams could only be measured with imprecision. Further, income is a more familiar concept than welfare and therefore may better convey relative rankings to policy makers.

OTA's new equivalence scale-adjusted measure relies on an additional assumption:

- Children are equivalent to adults: The equivalence scale adjusts for family size but makes no other adjustment for family composition. Children are assigned the same welfare level as the adults in the family. For example, a family composed of one adult and three children will have the same adjustment factor as a family of four adults. Some equivalent scales allow for differential adjustments for children. Other scales go further and make more refined adjustments by age.

III. Types of Equivalence Scales

There are two basic types of equivalent scales: scales based on equivalent needs and scales based on equivalent welfare. The equivalent needs approach considers the level of income necessary to achieve a minimal standard of living for a given family type. The U.S. poverty thresholds are an example of an equivalent needs scale. Equivalent welfare scales are based on traditional consumer theory and measure the level of income necessary to achieve the same level of welfare ("utility") across family types. In this approach, children increase the welfare of the family but also increase costs.

The equivalence scale OTA uses is based on the U.S. poverty thresholds, a well-known set of government statistics. Rather than use the U.S. poverty thresholds which show increasing returns to scale for small families and relatively constant returns to scale for large families, OTA follows Ruggles (1990) suggestion and uses a "smoothed" version of the poverty scale. Ruggles notes that a constant family size elasticity (FSE) scale of .5 appears to approximate the U.S. poverty thresholds.[1] Similarly, OTA's equivalence scale approximates the U.S. poverty thresholds but maintains increasing returns to scale across all family sizes by using a constant FSE.

Table 1 shows the U.S. poverty thresholds for 1998 (columns 1 and 2), and compares those thresholds to various constant FSE equivalence scales. The alternative scales vary from an FSE

---

[1] Family size elasticity (FSE) is the percent change in income for a percent change in family size.

=0 (columns 3 and 4) to an FSE=1 (columns 13 and 14), where FSE=0 represents the case of perfect returns to scale (no adjustment to income for family size) and FSE=1 represents the case of no returns to scale (per capita income equivalence). The FSEs for the scales between 0 and 1 are calculated by estimating what FSE would maintain the U.S. poverty threshold levels for each pair of thresholds given. Once the FSE is determined the remaining thresholds can be calculated.

For example, maintaining the U.S. poverty threshold levels for a family of size 1 and a family of size 2 would require a FSE of .35. The resulting thresholds and equivalence scale would appear as it does in columns 5 and 6. In columns 7 and 8, the relationship between families of size 1 and 3 is maintained and the FSE is .41. In columns 9 and 10, the relationship between families of size 2 and 3 is maintained and the FSE is .5. In columns 11 and 12, the relationship between families of size 2 and 4 is maintained and the FSE is .65.

IV. OTA's Equivalence Scale

OTA's equivalence scale is based on an FSE of .41. It will approximate the U.S. poverty thresholds for most people. An FSE of .5 is close to the average FSE across all poverty thresholds as Ruggles suggests, but the weighted average (weighted by the population) is closer to .41. An FSE of .41 by design exactly matches the poverty thresholds for families of size 1 and 3, and it closely matches the poverty threshold for families of size 2. Ninety percent of all families in 2000 are made up of 1, 2, or 3 members.

A constant FSE of .41 does not approximate the U.S. poverty thresholds for large families. A much higher FSE would be necessary to capture the large additional amounts of income allowed large families under the poverty thresholds. The divergence between OTA's equivalence scale and the U.S. poverty thresholds is due to OTA's scale showing smoothly increasing returns to scale while the U.S. poverty thresholds show a fairly constant return to scale for large families.

V. Comparing OTA's Scale to the Economic Literature on Equivalence Scales

Table 2 compares OTA's equivalence scale (constant FSE scale of .41) to other scales found in the literature. Some scales in the literature do not consider families of size 1. Instead they consider how the addition of a child affects the well-being of a couple. To facilitate comparison across scales, all scales have been adjusted so that they have the same 1.28 scale factor for a family of size 2. Scales are grouped into need-based and welfare scales, and the need-based scales are further subdivided according to the method used in the study. The Engel method considers necessity goods such as food to determine its scale. The Rothberg method considers the proportion of the budget devoted to adult goods such as alcohol. The surveys depend on subjective evaluations of well-being. Lazear and Michael assume a per capita measure for adults and then measure a child's equivalence to an adult.

OTA's equivalence scale is quite similar to the Rothberg method scales, survey scales, and all of the utility based scales. The Phipps (1998) utility scale is an exact match.

VI. Distribution of Income, Tax Burdens, and Families Using a FSE of .41

Table 3 shows the distribution of family economic income (FEI) and individual income and payroll taxes under OTA's current measure (FSE=0) and under alternative scales with constant FSEs. As the FSE increases to 1.0, the distributions for income and tax burdens become more equally distributed but not dramatically so. With an FSE of 0, 56.7 percent of FEI and 64.1 percent of income and payroll taxes accrue to the top quintile. With an FSE of 1.0, 52 percent of FEI and 58.4 percent of income and payroll taxes accrue to the top quintile. The difference between the income and tax distributions for an FSE of 0 and FSE of .41 are fairly small.

Tables 4a and 4b show the distribution of families by size across FEI quintiles. Table 4a shows the distribution with no adjustment for family size, OTA's current method. Table 4b shows the distribution of families adjusting the families using OTA's new equivalence scale (constant FSE of .41). The tables show that although the income and tax distributions are not significantly different overall, there are still some important movements across quintiles.

Under OTA's current method, the bottom quintile is disproportionately composed of singles (one person families). Singles account for 52.4 percent of all families but 65.1 percent of the bottom quintile. Under OTA's new scale, singles account for 54.3 percent of the bottom quintile. This difference in singles reflects the movement of large families lower in the income distribution. Under the OTA's new scale, 36.1 percent of five person families and 19.5 percent of "six-plus" person families are in the top quintile in the unadjusted distribution, but only 12.0 percent of five person families and 2.6 percent of six-plus person families are in the top quintile in the adjusted distribution.

These movements of families across income quintiles could be qualitatively important for distributional analyses of tax proposals that differentially affect large (or small) families. For example, a child-related tax benefit would likely appear more equally distributed across quintiles using OTA's new equivalence scale than under OTA's current measure.

Table 1: Poverty Thresholds for 1998 and Possible Equivalency Scales

Family Size	1998 poverty threshold		OTA's current measure		Maintain relation 1 & 2		Maintain relation 1 & 3		Maintain relation 2 & 3		Maintain relation 2 & 4		Per capita measure	
	Threshold (1)	Scale (2)	Threshold (3)	Scale (4)	Threshold (5)	Scale (6)	Threshold (7)	Scale (8)	Threshold (9)	Scale (10)	Threshold (11)	Scale (12)	Threshold (13)	Scale (14)
1	8,316	1.00	8,316	1.00	8,316	1.00	8,316	1.00	7,540	1.00	6,788	1.00	8,316	1.00
2	10,634	1.28	8,316	1.00	10,634	1.28	11,025	1.33	10,634	1.41	10,634	1.57	16,632	2.00
3	13,003	1.56	8,316	1.00	12,279	1.48	13,003	1.56	13,003	1.72	13,828	2.04	24,948	3.00
4	16,660	2.00	8,316	1.00	13,598	1.64	14,618	1.76	14,997	1.99	16,660	2.45	33,264	4.00
5	19,680	2.37	8,316	1.00	14,718	1.77	16,007	1.92	16,753	2.22	19,251	2.84	41,580	5.00
6	22,228	2.67	8,316	1.00	15,702	1.89	17,240	2.07	18,339	2.43	21,664	3.19	49,896	6.00
7	25,257	3.04	8,316	1.00	16,584	1.99	18,355	2.21	19,796	2.63	23,938	3.53	58,212	7.00
8	28,166	3.39	8,316	1.00	17,388	2.09	19,380	2.33	21,151	2.81	26,101	3.85	66,528	8.00
9	33,339	4.01	8,316	1.00	18,130	2.18	20,332	2.44	22,424	2.97	28,170	4.15	74,844	9.00
Family size "elasticity" (FSE)[1]			0		0.35		0.41		0.50		0.65		1.0	

1. FSE is calculated to solve the following:

$$\frac{\text{poverty threshold for a family of size x}}{(x)^{FSE}} = \frac{\text{poverty threshold for a family of size y}}{(y)^{FSE}}$$

E - 5

Table 2: Constant Family Size Elasticty of .41 Compared to Other Scales Found in the Literature[1]

		Need Based								Utility Based				
		Engel Method[3]			Rothberg Method[4]		Surveys[5]		Other[6]					
Family Size[2]	OTA's Equivalence Scale (Constant FSE of .41)	BLS (1982)	Deaton and Muelbauer (1986a)	Canadian (1986)	Deaton and Muelbauer (1986b)	Deaton, Castillo and Thomas (1989)	Danziger, Van der Gaag, Taussig, and Slomensky (1984)	DeVos and Garner (1989)	Lazear and Michael (1988)	Muelbauer (1977)	Van der Gagg and Slomensky (1982)	Johnson and Garner (1993)	Phipps (1998)	Ferreira, Buse, and Chavas (1998)
	(1)	(2)	(3)	(4)	(5)	(6)	(7)	(8)	(9)	(10)	(11)	(12)	(13)	(14)
1	1.00	0.91		0.94				0.93	0.64	0.92	1.00	0.72		
2	1.28	1.28	1.28	1.28	1.28	1.28	1.28	1.28	1.28	1.28	1.28	1.28	1.28	1.28
3	1.48	1.62	1.80	1.63	1.43	1.56	1.43	1.50	1.54	1.46	1.27	1.55	1.48	1.42
4	1.64	2.61	2.27	1.87	1.55		1.59	1.71	1.79	1.64	1.56	1.77	1.64	1.56
5	1.77	3.04		2.04			1.69	1.84	2.05		1.66	1.96		1.64

1. Some of the scales in the literature do not consider families of size 1. To facilitate comparison across scales, all the scales have been calibrated so families of size 2 are assigned 1.28 (the level found in column 1).

2. For the studies that only considered married couples (missing scale for family size of 1), size 2 families are composed of 2 adults and additions to family size are for children only.

3. The Engel method uses necessities such as food to determine the basis for equivalent needs.

4. The Rothberg method uses "adult" goods such as alcohol consumption to determine equivalent needs.

5. The surveys attempt to measure indirect utility through revealed preferences. They use subjective evaluations of consumption needs for families of different sizes.

6. Lazear and Michael (1988) measures the share of a family's budget alloted to children. They assume an additional adult's need is the same as the original adult and then estimate that each additional child will need 40 percent as much as an additional adult (no returns to scale).

Table 3: Percentage Distributions of Family Economic Income (FEI) and Individual Income and Payroll Taxes By Alternative Equivalence Scales

Equivalent FEI Quintile[1]	Current (fse=0)		fse=.35 (poverty 1&2)		fse=.41 (poverty 1&3)		fse=.5 (poverty 2&3)		fse=.65 (poverty 2&4)		fse=1.0 (per capita)	
	FEI	Individual Income and Payroll Taxes	FEI	Individual Income and Payroll Taxes	FEI	Individual Income and Payroll Taxes	FEI	Individual Income and Payroll Taxes	FEI	Individual Income and Payroll Taxes	FEI	Individual Income and Payroll Taxes
1	2.3	0.7	2.4	0.4	2.4	0.4	2.5	0.4	2.6	0.4	3.3	0.7
2	7.2	3.7	7.4	3.9	7.4	4.0	7.6	4.2	8.0	4.6	9.3	6.2
3	12.6	10.5	13.0	10.7	13.1	10.8	13.4	11.1	13.9	11.7	15.0	13.3
4	21.3	21.1	21.5	22.0	21.5	22.1	21.5	22.3	21.3	22.3	20.4	21.4
5	56.7	64.1	55.8	63.1	55.5	62.7	55.0	62.1	54.2	61.0	52.0	58.4
Total	100.0	100.0	100.0	100.0	100.0	100.0	100.0	100.0	100.0	100.0	100.0	100.0
80 to 94	27.2	30.2	26.7	29.6	26.6	29.4	26.3	29.1	25.9	28.4	24.8	26.8
95 to 99	14.7	15.9	14.4	15.7	14.4	15.6	14.2	15.5	14.0	15.2	13.5	14.6
top 1	14.8	17.9	14.6	17.8	14.6	17.7	14.5	17.6	14.3	17.4	13.8	16.9

1. Equivalent FEI equals (family of size x)/(x)^{fse}, where "fse" is the family size elasticity. For example, for a family of size 4, the divisor would be 1 if fse=0; 1.64 if fse=.35; 1.76 if fse=.41; 2.0 if fse=.5; 2.45 if fse=.65; and 4 if fse=1.

Table 4a: Distribution of Family Size by FEI-- e=0

Quintile	\ Number of persons in family						
	1	2	3	4	5	6+	Total

---- Family counts in thousands ---

Quintile	1	2	3	4	5	6+	Total
1	14,999	5,914	1,227	706	53	128	23,027
2	12,669	6,773	2,122	1,115	163	186	23,028
3	12,476	6,547	2,049	1,453	266	239	23,030
4	10,134	6,637	2,667	2,554	724	318	23,034
5	10,095	6,894	2,276	2,885	681	211	23,042
Total	60,373	32,765	10,341	8,713	1,887	1,082	115,161
top 15	7,417	4,980	1,838	2,297	549	193	17,274
top 4	2,165	1,460	362	486	118	16	4,607
top 1	513	454	76	102	14	2	1,161

---- percent distribution size across quintiles ---

Quintile	1	2	3	4	5	6+	Total
1	24.8	18.0	11.9	8.1	2.8	11.8	20.0
2	21.0	20.7	20.5	12.8	8.6	17.2	20.0
3	20.7	20.0	19.8	16.7	14.1	22.1	20.0
4	16.8	20.3	25.8	29.3	38.4	29.4	20.0
5	16.7	21.0	22.0	33.1	36.1	19.5	20.0
Total	100.0	100.0	100.0	100.0	100.0	100.0	100.0
top 15	12.3	15.2	17.8	26.4	29.1	17.8	15.0
top 4	3.6	4.5	3.5	5.6	6.3	1.5	4.0
top 1	0.8	1.4	0.7	1.2	0.7	0.2	1.0

---- percent distribution quintiles across size ---

Quintile	1	2	3	4	5	6+	Total
1	65.1	25.7	5.3	3.1	0.2	0.6	100.0
2	55.0	29.4	9.2	4.8	0.7	0.8	100.0
3	54.2	28.4	8.9	6.3	1.2	1.0	100.0
4	44.0	28.8	11.6	11.1	3.1	1.4	100.0
5	43.8	29.9	9.9	12.5	3.0	0.9	100.0
Total	52.4	28.5	9.0	7.6	1.6	0.9	100.0
top 15	42.9	28.8	10.6	13.3	3.2	1.1	100.0
top 4	47.0	31.7	7.9	10.5	2.6	0.3	100.0
top 1	44.2	39.1	6.5	8.8	1.2	0.2	100.0

Table 4b: Distribution of Family Size by FEI-- e=.41

Quintile	\multicolumn{6}{c}{Number of persons in family}	Total
	1	2	3	4	5	6+	Total

---- Family counts in thousands ---

Quintile	1	2	3	4	5	6+	Total
1	12,510	6,807	2,012	1,261	151	286	23,027
2	11,261	7,191	2,424	1,554	297	304	23,031
3	11,665	6,303	2,048	2,078	647	290	23,031
4	10,964	6,203	2,515	2,608	567	173	23,030
5	13,973	6,261	1,345	1,212	226	28	23,045
Total	60,373	32,765	10,344	8,713	1,888	1,081	115,164
top 15	10,209	4,794	1,104	955	189	25	17,276
top 4	3,076	1,094	197	206	32	3	4,608
top 1	688	373	44	51	5	0	1,161

---- percent distribution size across quintiles ---

Quintile	1	2	3	4	5	6+	Total
1	20.7	20.8	19.5	14.5	8.0	26.4	20.0
2	18.7	21.9	23.4	17.8	15.7	28.1	20.0
3	19.3	19.2	19.8	23.8	34.3	26.8	20.0
4	18.2	18.9	24.3	29.9	30.0	16.0	20.0
5	23.1	19.1	13.0	13.9	12.0	2.6	20.0
Total	100.0	100.0	100.0	100.0	100.0	100.0	100.0
top 15	16.9	14.6	10.7	11.0	10.0	2.3	15.0
top 4	5.1	3.3	1.9	2.4	1.7	0.3	4.0
top 1	1.1	1.1	0.4	0.6	0.3	0.0	1.0

---- percent distribution quintiles across size ---

Quintile	1	2	3	4	5	6+	Total
1	54.3	29.6	8.7	5.5	0.7	1.2	100.0
2	48.9	31.2	10.5	6.7	1.3	1.3	100.0
3	50.7	27.4	8.9	9.0	2.8	1.3	100.0
4	47.6	26.9	10.9	11.3	2.5	0.8	100.0
5	60.6	27.2	5.8	5.3	1.0	0.1	100.0
Total	52.4	28.5	9.0	7.6	1.6	0.9	100.0
top 15	59.1	27.8	6.4	5.5	1.1	0.1	100.0
top 4	66.8	23.7	4.3	4.5	0.7	0.1	100.0
top 1	59.3	32.1	3.8	4.4	0.4	0.0	100.0